# Gay Wedding Confidential

## Adventures and Advice from America's #1 Gay Wedding Planner

Bernadette Coveney Smith

iUniverse, Inc.
New York   Bloomington

# Gay Wedding Confidential
## Adventures and Advice from America's #1 Gay Wedding Planner

iUniverse books may be ordered through booksellers or by contacting:

iUniverse
1663 Liberty Drive
Bloomington, IN 47403
www.iuniverse.com
1-800-Authors (1-800-288-4677)

ISBN: 978-1-4502-4403-9 (sc)
ISBN: 978-1-4502-4405-3 (dj)
ISBN: 978-1-4502-4404-6 (ebk)

Printed in the United States of America

iUniverse rev. date: 12/29/2010

*For Jen, my lovable Leo who lights up every room.*

# Contents

Preface. . . . . . . . . . . . . . . . . . . . . . . . . . . . . . . . . . . . . . . . . . . .ix
Chronology: A gay marriage timeline . . . . . . . . . . . . . . . . . xvii
Chapter 1: Beginnings. . . . . . . . . . . . . . . . . . . . . . . . . . . . . . 1
Chapter 2: Getting Started . . . . . . . . . . . . . . . . . . . . . . . . . 13
Chapter 3: Involving Your Parents and Family. . . . . . . . . . . 32
Chapter 4: The Wedding Party . . . . . . . . . . . . . . . . . . . . . . . 39
Chapter 5: The Challenge in Coming Out . . . . . . . . . . . . . . 46
Chapter 6: What to Wear . . . . . . . . . . . . . . . . . . . . . . . . . . . 52
Chapter 7: Do You Need a Wedding Planner?. . . . . . . . . . . 63
Chapter 8: Choosing a Venue . . . . . . . . . . . . . . . . . . . . . . . . 71
Chapter 9: Plan On! Hotel Rooms, Wedding Web site,
   Save the Dates . . . . . . . . . . . . . . . . . . . . . . . . . . 83
Chapter 10: Lawfully Wedded. . . . . . . . . . . . . . . . . . . . . . . . 88
Chapter 11: From Trends to Traditions: The Gay Wedding
   Ceremony . . . . . . . . . . . . . . . . . . . . . . . . . . . . . . 94
Chapter 12: Showtime: Photos, Music, Makeup!. . . . . . . . . 125
Chapter 13: Dreaming in Logistics: Catering, Cake,
   Flowers, Transportation . . . . . . . . . . . . . . . . . . 139
Chapter 14: Fun With Paper: Your Wedding Invitations . . . 169
Chapter 15: Weddings on a Dime. . . . . . . . . . . . . . . . . . . . 180
Chapter 16: The Look, the Feel, the Flow!. . . . . . . . . . . . . . 184
Chapter 17: Designing Your Gay Wedding . . . . . . . . . . . . . 192
Chapter 18: Tying it Together Before You Tie the Knot. . . . 214
Chapter 19: Your Lives Together . . . . . . . . . . . . . . . . . . . . . 232
Appendix 1: Resources . . . . . . . . . . . . . . . . . . . . . . . . . . . . 236
Photograph Acknowledgements . . . . . . . . . . . . . . . . . . . . . 238

# Preface

On November 18, 2003, I was driving from my home toward the nearest subway stop, listening to National Public Radio. A news bulletin indicated that later that day, a decision in the case of *Goodridge v. the Massachusetts Department of Public Health* would be reached. This lawsuit was filed to remove the state's ban on same-sex marriage. At the time, I was three days removed from a Caribbean holiday with my girlfriend, and I was overcome with excitement.

I went to the office and glued myself to the Internet (constantly refreshing the screen!), waiting for the decision to be announced. Sometime around 11:00 AM, in my cramped little office with a view of the brick wall on the building across the street, I heard the news that the state may not "deny the protections, benefits, and obligations conferred by civil marriage to two individuals of the same sex who wish to marry."

The decision stated that marriages between same-sex partners would take effect in six months, on May 17, 2004.

Can you imagine the excitement? At the time, Canada was one of the few places in the world that let gay and lesbian couples legally marry. Our neighbor, Vermont, permitted something odd called "civil unions," which were separate from, and unequal to a legal marriage. But gay marriage! Legal! Here in Massachusetts! What a day!

If only it were that easy.

My job (that I mostly disliked) in downtown Boston was a few blocks from the grand old State House. Within the six-month period following the decision, there were almost daily rallies in support of or in opposition to gay marriage: those who opposed gay marriage wanted the legislature to preemptively ban it by law. I would frequently take long lunches to attend these rallies, listening to moving speeches from civil rights leaders like former state Senator Dianne Wilkerson and state Representative Byron Rushing and others. I stood alongside couples together twenty or thirty years, hoping they would one day marry.

I was inspired. You'd have to be coldhearted not to have been inspired. My day job was kind of boring, but my long lunches were so exciting. Experience had shown me that I was good at event planning, and lots of people said that I was "calm." And I had faith that the haters would not succeed in banning gay marriage before May 17, 2004. It was obvious from the crowds I saw that there would be tremendous pent-up demand for gay weddings and decided, "Hey! I'm going to be a gay-wedding planner!"

So I did. By March of 2004, I was the co-owner of a business called It's About Time. My website was up and I began teaching myself how to plan weddings. Within a week or two, I had my first clients, and I was planning weddings for that May, June, and beyond.

*Cambridge City Hall*

The city of Cambridge, Massachusetts, led by its openly gay mayor Ken Reeves, decided it wanted to be the first city in the United States to issue legal marriage licenses to same-sex couples, so it announced it would do so beginning 12:01 AM on Monday, May 17, 2004. Hundreds of couples lined up on the steps of Cambridge City Hall, flanked by supporters, a handful of protesters, and worldwide media. At 12:01 AM, the energy reached its climax as the doors opened.

My clients, Eve and Brenda, were the seventh couple in line. They paid their twenty-five dollar fee and were issued a voucher for their marriage license, which, according to the laws of the Commonwealth of Massachusetts, would be available for pick up in three days, unless they went to court (as many couples did) to apply for a waiver of this delay.

*Couples lined up inside waiting for their license*

*The scene on the steps of Cambridge City Hall*

On Tuesday, May 18, 2004, I received a call from a gentleman looking for help planning his gay wedding. I had five days to plan it.

A wedding in a week. They had the venue—a historic church. I needed to find a wedding cake, a photographer, flowers, an organist, and drinks. The vision was to have the wedding in a church with a cake and punch reception immediately following— the wedding and reception were open to all church members.

The ceremony was at First Church Boston, a Unitarian Church that performs same-sex marriages. One of the grooms was so excited that his was going to be the first gay wedding at this historic church that he wrote and distributed a press release. The couple took care of renting their tuxes and making dinner reservations afterward, but the bulk of the planning was up to me.

Within those six days, I hired vendors with whom I would later work routinely. The ceremony was very elegant and the grooms were stunningly handsome in their sharp black tuxes with their calla lily boutonnieres. All the vendors stepped up and did their jobs exceptionally well. My girlfriend and I cooked up a delicious punch concoction in the church's kitchen, which we served along with wedding cake to the guests, some of whom were perfect strangers to the grooms. All the guests were very well behaved.

That day I learned skills such as when and how to unroll an aisle runner, how to line up the members of the wedding party, and when to cue the organist for the processional.

I also discovered the pure joy of gay weddings—the feeling of extreme jubilation that is present among the guests. There's a feeling of anticipation, since many guests have never been to a gay wedding, and there's an inevitable lack of dry eyes during the ceremony because the sense of history in the room is unmistakable. The guests just know they are a part of something bigger than themselves.

*Gay weddings are different.* They are different in more ways than the gender of the engaged couple. They just feel different from heterosexual weddings, and every gay wedding is still making history. The guests at these weddings might not know it at the time, but gay weddings change the world, one beautiful marriage at a time, creating a powerful ripple effect that spreads to curious co-workers, neighbors and friends moved by the pure, simple power of love.

Fast-forward six years and Cambridge has been immortalized for issuing those licenses in the middle of the night. To this day, a quote from the State Supreme Court ruling hangs in Cambridge City Hall.

Last year, I had a gay couple travel from Pennsylvania to get married. I picked them up at their hotel in the morning and brought them to Cambridge City Hall to apply for their license. After that, I went with them to apply for a "marriage without delay" waiver at the courthouse, and when that was granted, we returned to City Hall to pick up their license.

All the while, I heard great stories about their families, their jobs, and the adorable story of how they met …

But the best part of the day (I think we'd all agree) was when we were in Cambridge City Hall, license in hand, with the Honorable Denise Simmons (justice of the peace and at that time, mayor of Cambridge). She officiated a beautiful, simple ceremony in her office and at the conclusion of the ceremony, presented my clients with a felt bag. Inside the bag was a key to the city of Cambridge.

Imagine the reaction of these two guys! They were elated! They were two African American men in their forties and at the time, Ms. Simmons was the only openly lesbian African American mayor of a city in the United States, handing them a key to her city. I didn't know it was coming—but what a pleasant surprise for all of us! I've worked with Ms. Simmons a number of other times and she always does a wonderful job, but that occasion was particularly special.

I feel by taking my clients to Cambridge, I'm treating them to a little piece of GLBT history.

In the seven years since that ruling, I have planned many weddings for a wide variety of fascinating couples, and I'll share some of their stories here. One of my favorite parts of the planning is getting a glimpse into the lives of incredible individuals, getting to know their families, their stories, and their tastes. On a very personal note, I was twenty-seven when I started It's About Time, so my own style choices and tastes were still evolving! It's always been fun meeting couples and thinking "hmm … do I want a high-powered life living in a chic urban loft with stunning contemporary art, or do I want an adorable suburban home full of light, the pitter-patter of baby feet and an organic veggie garden in the backyard?" It's a real treat meeting such an amazing variety of people every day.

This book is written for anyone who's planning a wedding, but especially those who are lesbian, gay, bisexual, and/or transgender. For the purposes of keeping things simple, I typically use the terms "gay wedding", "gay couples" and "brides" and "grooms". I know some of you are transgender and some lesbians don't identify as brides and so forth —but I'm not trying to be exclusive, I promise!

I've highlighted special tips that transgender brides or grooms may want to note, and I've also highlighted tips on planning a green wedding. There's also a chapter dedicated to saving money!

Thank you for reading this book. I wish you all the best in your journey together as a couple and with your wedding plans. I'm hopeful that my candid and practical approach will give you the tools to create a wedding that best reflects your personality and love for one another.

# Chronology: A gay marriage timeline

November 18, 2003: The Massachusetts Supreme Judicial Court gives the state legislature 180 days to enact same-sex marriage.

February 11, 2004: The Massachusetts General Court (the state legislature) completes the first step in a process that would ban same-sex marriage. The process is not continued.

February 12–March 11, 2004: The mayor of San Francisco, Gavin Newsom, orders City Hall to begin issuing marriage licenses to same-sex couples.

May 17, 2004: Same-sex marriage starts in Massachusetts.

August 12, 2004: The California Supreme Court rules that the San Francisco marriages authorized by Mayor Newsom are void.

September 29, 2005: California Governor Arnold Schwarzenegger vetoes a same-sex marriage bill that was approved by the legislature.

October 12, 2007: California Governor Arnold Schwarzenegger vetoes another same-sex marriage bill that was approved by the legislature.

May 15, 2008: The Supreme Court of California overturns the state's ban on same-sex marriage.

June 16, 2008: Same-sex marriage starts in California.

September 10, 2008: HB436, a bill that seeks to "eliminate the exclusion of same gender couples from marriage," is submitted to the New Hampshire House of Representatives.

October 10, 2008: The Supreme Court of Connecticut orders same-sex marriage legalized.

November 4, 2008: California voters pass Proposition 8, amending the state constitution to ban same-sex marriage.

November 5, 2008: Proposition 8 takes effect in California, stopping new same-sex marriage licenses from being issued after this date.

November 12, 2008: Same-sex marriage starts in Connecticut.

March 26, 2009: HB436 supporting same-sex marriage passes the New Hampshire House of Representatives.

April 3, 2009: The Iowa Supreme Court legalizes same-sex marriage.

April 6, 2009: A same-sex marriage bill is passed by the Vermont General Assembly and immediately vetoed by the governor.

April 7, 2009: The Vermont General Assembly overrides the governor's veto of the same-sex marriage bill, thereby authorizing same-sex marriage in Vermont.

Connecticut governor signs legislation that statutorily legalizes same-sex marriage (see Oct. 10 and Nov. 12, 2008), and also converts any existing civil unions into marriages as of October 1, 2010.

April 27, 2009: Same-sex marriage starts in Iowa.

April 29, 2009: HB436, supporting same-sex marriage, passes the New Hampshire Senate with minor amendments.

May 6, 2009: Maine Governor Baldacci signs Marriage Equality Bill. The New Hampshire House of Representatives concurs with the Senate's amendments to HB436, and the bill supporting same-sex marriage advances to Governor John Lynch.

May 12, 2009: A same-sex marriage bill passes in the New York Assembly (the state's lower house).

May 26, 2009: The California Supreme Court upholds Proposition 8, but also upholds the marriage rights of the 18,000 same-sex couples married while same-sex marriage was legal in that state,

June 3, 2009: The New Hampshire General Court (the state legislature) passes new HB73, which includes protections for religious institutions, as required by GovernorJohn Lynch to secure his signature on HB436, a bill legalizing same-sex marriage. Governor. Lynch signs both bills the same day.

September 1, 2009: Same-sex marriage starts in Vermont.

September 14, 2009: Same-sex marriage was scheduled to start in Maine, but was put on hold because enough signatures were collected to make the issue a ballot initiative.

November 3, 2009: Voters in Maine vote down gay marriage, therefore nullifying the law passed by the legislature and signed by the Governor.

December 15, 2009: The Washington, D.C. Council votes to legalize gay marriage and the bill is signed by Mayor Adrian Fenty three days later.

January 1, 2010: Same-sex marriage starts in New Hampshire.

March 3, 2010: Same-sex marriage starts in the District of Columbia

As of July 2010, these are the places in the United States where same-sex couples can legally marry:

- Connecticut
- District of Columbia
- Iowa
- Massachusetts
- New Hampshire
- Vermont

You've probably already thought about which state you'll marry in and here's a rundown of what's required in each state:

| State | Blood Test? | Witnesses? | Waiting Period? | Can waiting period be waived? | Fee? | How long is the license valid? |
|---|---|---|---|---|---|---|
| Connecticut | No | No | None | N/A | $35 | 65 days |
| District of Columbia | No | No | 3 days | Yes, in rare instances by a court order | $35 | No expiration date |
| Iowa | No | One | 3 days | Yes, in rare instances by a court order | $30 | 6 months |
| Massachusetts | No | No | 3 days | Yes, by a court order | Varies by city/town | 60 days |
| New Hampshire | No | No | None | N/A | $45 | 90 days |
| Vermont | No | No | No | N/A | $45 | 60 days |

Ensuring the recognition and protection of your family is critical—especially when you leave the state where you'll marry. We will talk more about protecting your family at the end of this book.

# Chapter 1:
# Beginnings

## My Beginnings

Here's my story: I had my very own gay wedding on July 3, 2009, in downtown Boston on Boston Harbor. I married the love of my life, Jennifer Coveney. She's beautiful! We met about two years prior, at a bar, and it was a love-at-first-sight kind of moment. That day was Jennifer's first day at a new job in Connecticut. She had returned to Boston that night to go out with friends and as fate would have it, I was there.

We had a whirlwind romance as many lesbian couples do, and within nine months, she had quit her job in Connecticut, took another in Boston and moved in with me. Have you heard the second-date joke?

What does a lesbian bring to her second date? A U-Haul!

That was us, almost!

Before Jen moved back to Boston, however, we'd been talking about marriage for a few months and knew that we were completely perfect for each other. We had had conversations about engagement ring styles and I had a sense of what she wanted. I even had an image printed off the Internet of what she liked. One day after I left a client's office in downtown Boston, I decided that, just for kicks,

I'd go ring shopping, and get a sense of what the cost might be and how difficult it would be to find the style she liked. (It should be noted that this is one of the parts of planning a wedding I'd never been involved in, since my clients almost always have the ring when I meet them! Prior to my turn, I'd never been ring shopping).

The second store I went to had the setting (which was a hybrid-tension setting) in stock, and the salesman showed me some diamond options. Before I knew it, I had committed to buying a ring. It happened so quickly and so easily, much more so than I expected. In the week or so that the ring was being made, I cooked up a number of elaborate and clever ways to propose. I was full of brilliant ideas but when I picked the ring up, I buried it in the back of my file cabinet and tried not to think about it—I wanted to wait a few months.

*Jen and I on our wedding day –*
*Jen is on the left and I am on the right*

A few weeks later, Jen moved in. That Sunday night, I made dinner (and it was appallingly bad). We sat in our pajamas, looking adoringly at each other when Jen took my hand and said, "I can't imagine being any happier than I am at this moment." I'm not sure what came over me—I think I saw her statement as a challenge—and politely excused myself to "get a sweater." I returned with the ring, mumbled something sweet, and before I knew it, we were engaged! Over burned steak!

Everyone has a different story and it's been fun watching my own unfold while working with others. One of my favorite parts of being a gay wedding planner is getting to know all kinds of couples and catching glimpses of their lives. I've worked with couples who've been together for thirty years living in the suburbs; couples who have kids and live on a quiet urban neighborhood street; couples who live in a downtown loft and have season tickets to the Celtics; and many couples who, like Jen and I, experienced love at first sight and didn't want to wait to begin the fun part of being together forever.

## Your Beginnings: Who Proposes and Who Gets the Ring?

Common question: With gay couples, does the person who was proposed to have to "propose back" with a ring?

With gay and lesbian couples, there's no right answer about who proposes, who gets a ring, and what that ring looks like.

*Andrew English's Fingerprint wedding bands*

I've seen rings that are a mirror images of each other, rings that had a fingerprint imprinted on them, rings that were formed from family jewelry; and simple platinum or steel bands. I've noticed that many lesbian couples don't want a "rock"—a big diamond engagement ring. I've seen femme lesbians present their butch partner with cuff links instead of an engagement ring. That's a very cool idea!

*Grooms with their diamond rings*

If you and your partner are talking about marriage, don't be afraid to have a conversation about the ring. It's better to know what your partner likes so you can be prepared.

In many cases, gay and lesbian couples have been together for so many years that they already own rings that symbolize the permanence of their relationship, and those are the rings that they will continue to wear after their marriage. Conversely, many couples that wear rings that are a symbol of their relationship choose to pick out new wedding bands together—bands that symbolize the next chapter in their lifetime journey. In my experience, couples who've been together for a while are less likely to have had a traditional "pop the question" proposal experience, and hence they don't buy or give engagement rings.

So while there is no standard "gay-engagement ring" or "gay-wedding band," this can be one of the first areas where you as a couple can express your personality through your wedding.

In my observation, many men will wear only one ring, not two. In this case, the engagement ring will often double as a wedding band.

I've found that younger lesbian brides (those under forty) are likelier to wear two rings. For example, my wife Jen, like many lesbians, wears her engagement ring and wedding band next to each other on the same finger. This is very common, and of course, traditional. My engagement ring doesn't have a stone (my choice), so my engagement ring is now on the ring finger of my right hand, and my wedding band is on the ring finger of my left hand.

Whatever decision you choose, walking into a jewelry store with your fiancée or fiancé looking for a wedding band can be intimidating to say the least, particularly if you would like a nontraditional band. Call around ahead of time to gauge the attitude of your local jewelers about working with same-sex couples. They may be great, or you may encounter an awkward pause, or even outright homophobia—but at least you are dealing with it on the phone rather than face-to-face. If you do have a great phone call, make sure you catch the name of that associate so that you can work with the right person when you stop by the store.

## A Marriage or a Wedding?

There have been twelve thousand same-sex marriages in Massachusetts since they became legal in 2004. During the six months that gay marriage was legal in California, there were eighteen thousand gay marriages! That's a lot for sure, but I know for certain that many of those couples had a simple marriage ceremony, not a big wedding. I met a couple recently that, like many couples, had a brief marriage at the Unitarian Universalist Arlington Street Church during the first week that they were legal in Massachusetts. At that point, the church was holding marriage ceremonies every fifteen minutes.

*Two grooms marrying at Arlington Street Church the first week gay marriage was legal in Massachusetts*

My company provides wedding planning services – but it also provides marriage planning services for those who simply want to make it legal. Whatever you choose, there's a good reason for each.

I've seen the "marriage vs. wedding" debate arise among couples, especially those who grew up thinking it would never be possible to marry, or who've never envisioned their own wedding. I've met many couples that are unsure whether they want a wedding, or in which one partner is trying to convince the other on the subject. In the beginning, back in 2004, many couples I worked with were in their forties and fifties and there was enormous pent up demand for the legal right to marry. Some of those couples in their forties and fifties rushed to marry right away because they were afraid the right was going to be taken away.

Now that gay marriage is secure in the six places it's legal in the United States, it's become normalized, like the next logical step in a relationship, just like our straight counterparts. And with that, I've seen the average age of my clients drop to their early thirties, which is around my age and the average age of many marrying couples in general.

So what do you do, have a marriage ceremony or have a wedding? Jen and I can relate. We were talking about this topic when discussing how our wedding planning would have gone if I hadn't been a wedding planner. She said that she would have tried to convince me to have an elopement; just the two of us. I said that even if I hadn't been a planner, I'd never have gone along with that: having my friends and family witness and validate my marriage was way too important to me.

*One of my elopement clients right after their wedding*

Of course, weddings cost a lot of money, typically between twenty thousand and thirty-five thousand dollars, depending of course on the number of guests. I have a lot of experience with weddings and there is nothing more moving to me, still, to this day, than seeing a gay or lesbian couple stand up in front of their friends and family and get legally married. The validation and support they receive from their guests is truly priceless. The key word is *validation*. Gay weddings are jubilant. There is a sense of triumph. And there is *no greater party*.

I understand the desire to elope or to keep the event small. Many brides or grooms don't like being the center of attention or simply can't or don't want to spend the money or deal with the planning stress. And I'll never try to convince a couple otherwise. The validation of one's community isn't something everyone needs.

## What is Normal?

One of the questions I often get from couples and clients (and reporters and anyone curious about gay weddings) is, "what's normal?" "What does a gay wedding look like?" This is one of the reasons I developed a seminar for engaged same-sex couples and another seminar for those in the wedding industry hoping to work with them—and it's the main reason for this book!

Every time gay marriage becomes legal in a new place, this question arises over and over. Couples never expected the day would come and don't know what to do to prepare or how to make their wedding special. In fact, I went to an event recently where I heard a story of an Iowa couple who came to Massachusetts to get married one week before the ruling legalizing gay marriage in Iowa was issued. I know that when many same-sex couples in Iowa began applying for their marriage licenses, they were thinking, "now what?" "How the heck do I plan a gay wedding?"

You should know that any wedding, gay or straight, should be about the personality and style of the couple. Don't let anyone tell you differently. The fundamental decisions are the same regardless of the couple's orientation. You have to think about how much to spend, who to invite, what kind of celebration to have, and where to have it.

## The Inevitable Wedding Stress

Wedding planning can create emotional havoc. Even when you're a wedding planner! (Possibly especially when you're a wedding planner!)

Throughout our engagement, it became increasingly odd for me to be on the other side of wedding planning and to go through so many of the same issues that my clients face. My concerns and emotions were not issues specific to a gay wedding; rather, they were issues any couple may go through.

My parents passed away over nine years ago, so the planning was always a little bittersweet for me. Jen's mom came to town to go dress shopping with her. That's a timeless rite of passage that I relied on the kindness of my friends to experience with me (once I finally figured out what to wear).

All of my family lives out of state or out of the country, so only those in my immediate family were invited to our bridal shower, and from that short list only my sister actually came. Jen's family, on the other hand, lives mostly in Massachusetts, so our shower guests were mostly friends and Jen's family. My sister can hold her own and I was grateful that she was there, but it made me sad that she came alone. It also makes me enormously grateful to be blessed with amazing friends and for marrying into a family that completely embraces and supports me.

Like many brides, I was anxious about who from my family would come to the wedding. I invited dozens of cousins, aunts, and uncles from around the world but had zero sense as to who from my entirely Irish-Catholic family would make the trip to Boston for my gay wedding. When it was all said and done, I was lucky to have great representation from both sides of my family, with many cousins making the trip and even a few elderly aunts. But the anticipation was a killer.

I have a client whose wedding planning is on hiatus because the brother of a bride recently died, and there's no joy in planning after such a major loss.

The trick is preparing for a wedding as a celebration, to allow yourself to experience the joy of what you have and what you are creating, while finding whatever way you can to acknowledge the journey. Memorializing the path that you're on is something that a skilled officiant can do as part of the ceremony, and I'll touch on that later.

## Wedding Nightmares

I've been joking that I need to start carrying around nips of liquor in my emergency kit: sometimes my brides and grooms get really nervous! It's actually very cute ... but I can relate. Yes, I am a very calm person, but it's strange how nerves manifest themselves.

During my engagement, I dreamt this highly implausible dream that had little basis in reality: our ceremony and reception were across the street from one another, but that street was a very busy road in Cambridge, Massachusetts. Guests had to walk across this traffic-filled road in severe heat. To enter the reception site, there was a very long, gradual, ascending stairway, followed by a trap door down! The reception began with no cocktail hour, and Jen and I were immediately seated. The cheesy, 70s-era disc jockey who came with the wedding package introduced some live musicians, one of whom did a Kurt Cobain tribute (in costume), and another who sang folk music. I then left the reception because I forgot something back at the ceremony site, and by the time I returned, everyone was standing around for cocktail hour but I missed all the food. Let me tell you: it was a lot of pressure planning a wedding when your career is a wedding planner. A lot. The expectations of guests, acquaintances, clients, vendors, colleagues, and followers on Twitter were very high. Even without this kind of pressure, Jen experienced anxiety on the verge of panic attacks—but her stress came while she was awake.

My point is that I can relate to clients' and friends' stories of wedding nightmares. One of my clients had a nightmare that her fiancée left her, saying, "I just want to be friends." Another wrote, "I dreamt about the wedding again last night. This time, it was a *requirement* that we both wore veils and I was not happy."

It's horrifying what the subconscious creates.

## Bridezillas!

I am hereby giving you permission to be a Bridezilla (or a Groomzilla)!

I look at it this way: you're probably spending tens of thousands of dollars on your wedding day. You want it to be perfect. You want to do this only once.

Add to that moms or future mother-in-laws who have strong opinions (and may be paying for a portion of the wedding). You may encounter dear friends who themselves are showing 'zilla tendencies. You may suddenly have a lot of extra pressure at work. You may want to lose weight for the wedding. You may be very upset by your wedding gown alterations (Jen knows all about this one ...)

You can be a 'zilla. Those of us in the wedding industry don't mind. And we know better than to take it personally.

Honestly, I understand, and Jen and I have each had our own 'zilla moments in the course of planning our own wedding. Weddings are stressful and get many people around you excited! You are probably going to get lots of unsolicited advice and opinions, and if you are a LGBT couple, you're probably going to get lots of advice from straight friends and family who will tell you how a wedding should look and feel based on their own experiences with straight weddings.

Stand your ground. It's your wedding, and your vision. I'd hate for you to lose sight of that, and to lose part of your identity in the process (even if this means that you sometimes act like a 'zilla.) You don't have to apologize for it, certainly not to wedding professionals. At some point in every planning process, I hear from one partner, "I'm sorry, I'm having a 'zilla moment" or "I went so 'zilla on my mother last night." I'd much rather have that happen than have a couple upset that their vision has been compromised. If you're my client, I take it all in stride.

Rock on, 'zillas!

# Chapter 2:
# Getting Started

This book will mirror the method I use with clients when we plan a wedding. We start with the five Ws and the H:

Who: Who are you inviting?
Why: Why did you choose to invite the people you chose to invite?
What: Um, your wedding, right...
When: When is the wedding?
Where: Where is the wedding?
How: How will it look, feel, taste, smell, and sound?

## First Things First: Create a System

It's very important to have a system in place so you stay organized (and don't lose your mind!) through this very stressful wedding planning process. A sensible, easy-to-use system is a must.

You can go out and buy a binder or one of those wedding planning kits, but the reality is that most communication with vendors and venues happen by email, so the old-fashioned kits aren't particularly useful.

I, and most of my clients, use online planning tools. The easy, free way to do this is through Google Docs. If you go online with any web browser, visit www.Google.com and sign up for an email account. Once you have an email account, you can go to Docs. Google.com and upload some of your own wedding planning files.

Even better, Google Docs actually has wedding-planning templates that you can download and use to help tackle the following tasks:

- Manage your guest list
- Create your budget
- Manage your to-do list
- Manage your "day of" wedding schedule
- Create a seating chart
- Create a music list for the DJ or band
- Create organizer spreadsheets for photographers, stationers, venues, hotels, florists, hair and makeup, caterer, cake and more.

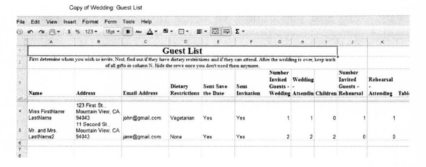

The documents can be shared in a central online private directory, so you and your partner can both view them, edit them, and access them from any web browser. It couldn't be more convenient and is a green option for wedding planning. As I mentioned earlier, most vendor communication happens by email, and your vendor contracts, forms, and schedules can all be kept in the same shared folder for 24/7 access. You can also save inspirational photographs, and create your own inspiration boards and images, and save them into this same Google Docs area.

## Choosing a Date

How do you figure out when to get married? My advice may be contrary to other planners, but I always encourage couples to have an open mind about their wedding date.

- Blackout dates. Start with a specific month or two, and ask your closest guests to tell you any blackout dates within that time frame. For example, a mom of a bride may already be booked to attend a major work conference. Once you've eliminated blackout dates, rank your top three available dates. Use this when venue shopping, so you can have the greatest number of options. I'd hate for you to not be able to marry in your dream venue because it's already booked. Flexibility in your wedding date can help avoid that problem.
- Travel arrangements. Choose a date that gives your guests at least six months to make travel arrangements, if necessary. They may have to arrange to take time off of work and for childcare. Those coming in from other places will need time to get the best airfare. Bottom line: give your guests a reasonable amount of notice!
- Weather concerns. Keep in mind any climate or seasonal factors that may affect your wedding plans. For example, if you are dreaming of an outdoor wedding, do some research on the months with the lowest amount of precipitation. Obviously, if you live in a hurricane zone, you will want to consider a date outside of hurricane season. If you are getting married in states with four distinctive seasons, be prepared for

freezing weather during winter months and the travel challenges of ice and snow.
- Holiday weekends. Holiday weekends have pros and cons for weddings. They give you the option of having a Saturday or Sunday wedding but may bring with them a premium for airfare, hotels, and/or paying for child and pet-care. Major holidays (such as Thanksgiving and Christmas) may bring with them premium charges from vendors who aren't able to spend that time with their own families.
- Avoiding prime dates. Keep in mind that an off-season, Friday or Sunday date can give you leverage in negotiating discounts with vendors.

Although your own wishes are important, please please keep your guests in mind when choosing a date.

## Day or Evening?

Do you want an evening affair or are you thinking of a daytime wedding?

There are pros and cons to both evening and daytime celebrations. The overall guest experience will vary depending on the time of day. Be aware that guests are more inclined to dance at night, if you are imagining a lot of dancing at your wedding.

The time of day of your event can have a significant impact on your food budget. Guests generally drink less at daytime events and if you are having a daytime event, you can serve brunch-type food. Don't you know how cheap eggs are?! Because some couples would rather not serve alcohol (perhaps they or they families sober), daytime weddings are great because those guests who are not sober are less likely to want alcohol. One of our first weddings was of two ladies who wanted to create a "Great Gatsby/lawn party"-type vibe. The wedding began at 11:00 AM, and As you see in the photo, I think they were successful in bringing their theme to life!

*The Gatsby inspired wedding*

## Create a Guest List

Once you've selected your top three dates, you can begin to think about who to invite.

Wedding drama is certainly inevitable. We must accept that as fact. Family issues, budget stress, decision-making challenges … but nothing seems to cause more anxiety than who to invite, and perhaps more importantly, who not to invite.

Creating a guest list should be one of the first things you do once you're ready to plan your wedding. I tell my clients to invite only people who will be thrilled to support them. In some cases, especially with family, this is easier said than done.

I had clients who were torn up because one of their aunts had signed an anti-gay marriage petition. (Her name was found on KnowThyNeighbor.org, a website that provided this information.) The aunt was invited anyway. I am hopeful that witnessing that beautiful wedding changed her heart and mind (as it often does). The reality is that not everyone in the world is happy about your gay wedding.

It's difficult knowing where to draw the line with your wedding-guest list, but you have to. Not only will the number of guests have budget implications but it will have an impact on your options when it's time to go venue shopping!

Many couples find themselves having to invite friends or co-workers of their parents that they don't know very well (if at all). My best piece of advice is to create guest-list policies and be consistent with them. Start by asking yourselves the following questions – I call them "policy decisions:"

- Work backward from your budget. If at least half of your budget will go toward food and beverages, how many people can you afford to host?
- Are ex-boyfriends and ex-girlfriends invited? I know the lesbians tend to *love* to keep in touch with their exes!
- Do you invite friends you haven't talked to in three or more years if the friendship has grown apart?
- Do you have to invite everyone whose wedding you attended, even if it was many years ago and the friendship hasn't survived?
- Do your work colleagues get invited?
- What about friends from high school and college that you've reconnected with via Facebook or another social networking site?
- Do you invite children? Do you let babies come?
- Do you ask your single friends to bring a guest? (a plus-one in *Sex and the City* speak). What if they are in a serious relationship but not living together? What if they are in a serious relationship and living together? What if they seem to have no hope of being in a serious relationship any time soon?
- Are friends and neighbors of your parents invited? Your parents may want to honor some of their dearest friends with an invitation—but then again, some parents don't want to draw attention to their child's gay wedding.
- Are your parents' work colleagues invited?

A couple of etiquette notes: if someone is invited to your shower, he or she has to be invited to your wedding. This rule applies no matter who hosts the shower—family, attendants, or friends. If your work colleagues also throw you a shower, that doesn't mean they need a wedding invitation. Thank them at the event and immediately send them thank-you notes.

Some people will advise you to have an A list and a B list of invitations. The A list are the people who absolutely must get an invitation. The B list is the backup list. To do this successfully:

- The number of people on the A list should be no higher than the maximum capacity of your venue.
- Your B list should rank guests in order of priority.
- If someone from the A list can't make it, then you send an invitation to the next name on the B list the day after you receive the declination.
- Send out the invitations early enough so that if someone from the A list can't make it, the person on the B list doesn't realize that he or she was an afterthought!

It's a little bit tacky but lots of people do it. You just have to do it right.

In the case of my own wedding, I'm sorry to report that I didn't come upon the perfect answer. I can only empathize and let you know that I've gone through the same thing. In our case, because of the maximum capacity of the venue and because I wanted to invite my vast extended family, we hit limitations. We decided not to invite work colleagues or parents' friends, and with a few exceptions, only invited friends who were currently active in our lives. I felt strongly about including some people from my past (who live out of state) who saw me through difficult times, and/or were a role model to me. And that meant that others didn't make the cut. It seems almost impossible not to offend someone.

So, how do you draw the line in peace, without feeling unduly judged? Make your policy decisions and stick to them! If you do, at least your integrity will be intact.

Once you've created the parameters of your invitees, make your list. If that list is still higher than what your budget allows, then start removing people one at a time, and if you must, add them to a B list who will get invitations once those from the A list declinations.

When we were planning our wedding, I realized that I'd been unfriended as a Facebook friend by someone who knew about the wedding but did not get invited. We had once been close (there was no dramatic falling-out, just a circumstance-related growing apart). It hurt, but I must have hurt her. And unfortunately, there is the rub.

## Making a Wedding Budget

When I work with a new client, one of the first things we do is create a budget—a very specific, line-item budget. The budget I use is has two categories, variable expenses and fixed expenses. The items under variable expenses (such as food) change as the number of your wedding guests changes. The fixed expenses (such as photography) do not change as your guest count changes.

You don't have to have a wedding planner to make a chart like the one below, which I created in Microsoft Excel. The Per Person/Piece column relates to variable expenses.

# Wedding Budget Chart

| | Per Person/ Piece | Estimated Cost | Actual Cost |
|---|---|---|---|
| **VARIABLE EXPENSES** | | | |
| | | | |
| Save-the-Date Cards | | | |
| Postage | | | |
| Invitations | | | |
| Postage | | | |
| Rehearsal Dinner | | | |
| Welcome Gifts | | | |
| Parking | | | |
| Coat Check | | | |
| Ceremony Program | | | |
| Food and Service Staff - Assumes Hors d'oeuvres and 3–4 Course Dinner | | | |
| Alcohol and Bar Service - Assuming Full Open Bar | | | |
| Admin Fee + Gratuity for Food and Beverage | | | |
| Cake | | | |
| Favors | | | |
| Menu | | | |
| Seating Cards | | | |
| Subtotal A | | | |
| | | | |
| **FIXED EXPENSES** | | | |
| Hotel Room | | | |
| Officiant Fee | | | |
| Ceremony Space Rental (if a House of Worship) | | | |

| | | | |
|---|---|---|---|
| Ceremony and Cocktail Hour Music | | | |
| Transportation | | | |
| Bouquets | | | |
| Corsages/Boutonnieres | | | |
| Ceremony Arrangements | | | |
| Reception Rental | | | |
| Wardrobe Partner A | | | |
| Wardrobe Partner B | | | |
| Wedding Planner | | | |
| Wedding Rings | | | |
| Hair and Makeup | | | |
| Photographer | | | |
| Photography albums | | | |
| Videographer | | | |
| Centerpieces | | | |
| Disc Jockey or Band | | | |
| Tent | | | |
| Dance Floor | | | |
| Specialty Linens | | | |
| Tables and Chairs | | | |
| Place Settings | | | |
| Guest Book | | | |
| Cake Knife and Server | | | |
| Toasting Flutes | | | |
| Attendant Gifts | | | |
| Lighting/Other Decorations | | | |
| Subtotal C | | | |
| | | | |
| **Grand Total** | | | |

You may not be purchasing or renting everything on the above list. For example, you may choose a venue where tables, chairs, tent, and dance floor rental are not necessary. This is simply a comprehensive list of wedding expenses so you can be fully informed of the possibilities.

Make a budget and stick to it, to the best of your ability.

Think a lot about your taste and style. If you have Abercrombie taste on an Old Navy budget, then you should invite fewer guests, have a destination wedding—or even elope! There are more tips in the chapters ahead on how to save money on your wedding.

# Planning Timeline:

Clip this checklist and use it as your guide as you go through the planning process.

Twelve+ months before the wedding:

- Make your guest list.
- Build your wedding budget.
- Hire a wedding planner to help you with the vendor-selection process.
- Compare facilities for ceremony, rehearsal, and reception sites.
- Set your wedding date, time, and location.
- Interview and hire an officiant.
- Identify attendants, ushers, and the like.
- Identify a hotel for room-blocks for out-of-town guests

Six to twelve months before the wedding:

- Create a wedding website.
- Order and mail save-the-date cards.
- Set up gift registry.
- Choose a theme, if you like, to be integrated throughout the wedding (you might choose a color theme, or something more specific, like an ocean theme or a Broadway musical theme).
- Compare and hire vendors who may work only one event a day and set aside money for deposit checks:
  o Photographer.
  o Entertainment.
  o Videographer.
  o Hair and Makeup Artists.

- Compare and hire vendors who may work multiple events per day and set aside money for deposit checks:
  o Caterers.
  o Florists.
  o Rental party services for chairs, tents, and the like.
  o Bakers.
- Select Your Wardrobe:
  o Select partners' and attendants' clothing.
  o Mothers' clothing choices to coordinate with wedding, if desired.
- Schedule an engagement photo shoot with your photographer.
- Choose Your stationery.
  o Select invitations.
  o Select stationery for thank-you notes.

Two to three months before the wedding:

- Decide:
  o Music for wedding and reception.
  o Location and guest list for rehearsal dinner.
  o Choose a final menu with caterer.
- Address and stamp envelopes and mail invitations.
- Confirm:
  o Confirm flower orders, rose petals, confetti, etc.
  o Confirm wedding cake flavors.
- Buy:
  o Gifts for all attendants.
  o Wedding favors.
  o Wedding rings.
- Arrange:
  o Transportation for wedding party.
  o Hair and makeup trials.

- o Ceremony microphone and sound system, if necessary.
- o Special champagne toasting flutes if desired.
- o Special cake knife and server, if desired.

One month before the wedding:

- Make the following arrangements:
  - o Get floor plans of venues.
  - o Decide on seating arrangement for reception.
  - o Confirm hotel accommodations and honeymoon tickets.
  - o Determine places for partners to dress.
  - o Determine places for attendants to dress.
  - o Apply for and pick up marriage license.
- Get clothing ready:
  - o Break in shoes.
  - o Check final fittings on clothing for the partners.
- Sit for wedding portrait.
- Write announcement for paper.
- Attend pre-wedding showers and parties.

Two weeks before the wedding:

- Confirm and notify:
  - o Verify number of wedding guests.
  - o Inform caterer of final number and any special dietary needs.
- Print!
  - o Design and print a program booklet for ceremony.
  - o Design and print menus for each table.
  - o Design and print place cards for each table or escort cards.

One week before the wedding:

- Prepare a full day-of schedule.
- Confirm vendors:
  o Officiant.
  o Photographer.
  o Videographer.
  o Florist.
  o Musicians.
  o Baker.
  o Favor supplier.
  o Rental company.
  o Make final preparations:
- Pack for honeymoon.
  o Spend at least one quiet evening with each other.
  o Make decisions and purchases about personal touches—votives in bathrooms, rose petals, etc.
  o Designate someone to transport gifts and flowers from the reception.
  o Designate someone to pin personal flowers.
  o Buy guest book.
  o Write a speech or thank-you words, if desired.

The day before the wedding:

- Lay out partners' clothing
- Pack partners' going away clothing.
- Pack toiletries.
- Make out final checks to the officiant, musicians, DJ, photographer, caterer, and any other vendors due a final payment.
- Put aside envelopes for tips for catering staff, musicians, officiant, and drivers.
- Attend rehearsal dinner.

The day of the wedding:

- Get dressed.
- Thank everyone for attending and helping.
- Let your wedding planner distribute the checks; manage the flow; answer all questions; place the place cards, menus, and favors; and do all setup and cleanup!

After the wedding:

- Mail wedding announcements, if you use them.
- Write remainder of thank-you notes.
- Invite family and wedding party as dinner guests.
- Live, love, laugh, and be happy!

## The Gay-Wedding Registry

Are you registering for gifts? It seems like the answer should obvious, but in fact, many gay couples do not. The top two reasons for not registering that I've observed are:

- Many gay couples have already been together for years, accumulating a houseful of great stuff—and just don't need to register.
- Many gay couples would rather their guests support an important charity, such as those that fight for marriage equality everywhere, rather than give them gifts.

However, many more couples *do* register for gifts, assuming that inasmuch as most people are going to give them stuff anyway, it should be stuff they actually want, right? Be aware, however, that while most guests give a gift to the couple, they are not obligated to do so, and you should never expect one.

You should note that most stores are still very heterosexist when it comes to wedding registries. There's a good chance you'll see "bride's name" and "groom's name" on paperwork and on websites. There may be assumptions made about your relationship if you go to the store in person to register for items. The salesclerk might not be enthusiastic. The good news is that the most popular stores allow you to set up your registry online if you would prefer to do so.

So how do you appropriately create a registry?

As a couple, make a list of what you need to furnish and decorate your home. Plan out décor and colors. What is your style: contemporary, traditional, country, or something else?

- Register for more items than you actually need. Guests like choices and you're not going to get everything on your list. Put yourself in your guests' situation: if all that's left on the registry is an iron and a spatula set, they won't have any fun shopping for you. Plus, lots of stores will help you fulfill your gift registry by offering you a discount on the remaining items after the wedding.

- Register for gifts across a spectrum of budgets, so your guests have options depending on what they can afford. (Don't make assumptions about people's generosity [or lack thereof]. You'll be surprised by who gives what!) This is also important because if you do have a wedding shower, you'll likely get lower-priced gifts at that event and more generous gifts for your wedding.

- Register at multiple stores to give your guests an option that is comfortable for them. For example, even if you register for lower-priced items at Saks, some guests won't even bother to look there, so also include a more budget-friendly option like Target.

- Remember that it is never good etiquette to include registry information with your wedding invitations. However, this information may be included on shower invitations or you may link to the registries on your wedding website. And you can include the wedding website URL on a logistics card that is enclosed with your invitation suite.

- Provide the store with an address where gifts can be sent. Your guests will like having the option of not bringing the physical gifts to the wedding.

- Consider registering through a charity like the Human Rights Campaign (HRC). Guests can make a donation in your name and feel good about their choice.

- Yes, you can register for a honeymoon if you wish. Some honeymoon registries double as travel agents so you can book your plans directly through them.

Others, like Honeyfund, are merely vessels by which you receive checks from your guests. You can indicate where you are going and outline what you may do while you are there. Guests may, for example, treat you to a spa visit, a sailing expedition, dinner on the beach, or a guided tour through a rainforest. It's a nice win-win. Your guests feel like they are contributing to your honeymoon and they are (and the money you receive that is earmarked for a particular activity may be used in any way you like.)

# Chapter 3:
# Involving Your Parents and Family

Your parents may be thrilled for you when you announce that you're marrying a person of the same gender, but keep in mind that some parents will freak out. I've seen my share of both situations and have talked with numerous couples for whom the parental reaction is a big stressor. One of my clients related:

*My mom seemed to be really trying to prepare us for the possibility that my Dad wouldn't be coming to the wedding. He didn't talk about it and didn't acknowledge it at all while we were there this weekend, and when she tries to make plans he says he doesn't want to talk about it. My take on it is that we will have a beautiful, memorable wedding with or without him, and I'm going to put all my focus and energy into enjoying the rest of our planning and getting excited for the big day.*

But this isn't a chapter about coming out to your parents or dealing with their acceptance or rejection. Chances are you've already done that. I'm not here to talk about religion or politics. I'm here to talk about getting your parents excited for your gay wedding!

Some parents have a hard time with the idea of gay marriage, even if they support your relationship. To some, a gay marriage may not seem real because it may not be sanctioned in the state where they live. And if you're like Jen and I, and some of our clients, the relationship may have been a whirlwind one and the engagement may have come fairly quickly.

Whatever the case, the question is, how do you get your parents excited about your gay wedding?

In our own situation, Jen did not get the reaction she had hoped for from her parents. They were a bit stunned. In all fairness, Jen had been engaged to a woman before (in her wild youth) but now Jen was a grown-up, in her thirties, and she had found me. (And I'm very lovable!) But her parents were less than thrilled. Why?

I've talked to Jen's parents about their ambivalence, and a large part of their feelings is related to the fact that as Maryland residents, gay marriage is not something that's on their radar. It doesn't seem possible to them. Yet here in Massachusetts and in a few other states, it is. We're used to it. They are not.

## Step One: Be Patient

Don't get bent out of shape if your parents are less enthusiastic than you'd hoped. Give them time. Don't get defensive and bitter. Remember that it may have taken you a while to get used to the idea (of being gay or of getting married), so be patient with their process. Your parents may feel like your wedding plans are a runaway train. They may feel like you got engaged out of the blue, are furiously planning and they're left at the station wondering what the heck just happened. I recall Jen being frustrated and angry with her parents for not being more excited about our wedding. I urged her to have patience. She had no choice. Jen's parents are incredibly kind people and came around, of course.

## Step Two: Slowly Share Your Excitement

Gradually start sharing your excitement about the wedding plans. Say things like, "we took a look around at venues today and it was really fun," or "I've been looking through bridal magazines for dresses I might like." This one works great: "I received the sweetest engagement card in the mail today from Aunt Mary! She sounds so excited for us!" My advice is to just say normal, typical, wedding-planning things, as if it's any other conversation with your parents. Don't make a big deal out of the plans at first but start to plant the seed that your wedding is for real and that you are taking action.

This is what I urged Jen to do with her mom. Slowly start releasing information about your ideas, just in the normal course of conversation. It piques curiosity.

## Step Three: Ask for Advice

Asking for advice not financial help (yet) is the most critical step. Ask open-ended questions about etiquette issues, like who to invite. An example would be, "should we invite all of our second cousins to the wedding?" Or ask for advice about logistical matters: "we're thinking of having an outdoor ceremony. What do you think of that?" You want to involve your parents without generating guilt.

In our case, Jen asked her mom for ideas on which of her parents' friends to invite, and whether her grandma could make the trip. These types of questions might strike your parents personally, and may make them feel a little guilty.

## Step Four: Invite Greater Participation

Over time, invite your parents to participate in more emotional wedding-planning issues. I believe that excitement is contagious, and if you are excited about your wedding, eventually your parents will be too. You'll start to know when is the time to recruit them to be actively involved—and if you are a bride, there is no greater opportunity than dress shopping (if you are wearing a dress) with your mother. If you are not wearing a dress, ask for your mom's help with choosing someone to do a reading during the wedding ceremony or about her favorite flowers. Invite the input of the partners' mothers and show excitement over their responses.

Shopping for a dress became a turning point for Jen in our wedding plans. This is where Jen's parents boarded the Coveney-Smith wedding train. Her mom came to town and they went dress shopping. Jen started talking about the bridal shower. During her visit, Jen's mom visited the place where we were to marry and loved it. And when she went back home, she was filled with excitement. Jen's dad then got excited too and the Coveney-Smith wedding train started to pull out of the station.

## Step Five: Ask for Money

Once you've got your parents excited and engaged and sharing their ideas and etiquette advice, ask for money. Obviously, do this only if your parents have some reasonable capacity to contribute. Use your best judgment. But if you do so, the easiest way to do it is to complain about money, "I didn't know how much a wedding was going to cost." And here's the best one, some variation of, "I don't think we can invite the cousins, your friends from work, and/or your next-door neighbors, because we just can't afford it."

If your parents bite and are willing to contribute, I'd advise asking for a specific dollar amount, rather than for coverage of certain expenses. The reason is that if you ask them to pay for the band and the photographer, your parents might feel like they get to select those vendors. And you don't want to relinquish that control. This is your vision.

Jen said priceless gems such as, "even though Bernadette's a wedding planner, it's still crazy how much things cost when it's your own wedding!" Jen's parents were very generous.

## Step Six: Give your Parents a Project

Channel your parents' new enthusiasm into a very narrow and specific project. This is very important if you want to retain ownership over your wedding plans. The goal is to engage your parents with something they would strive to be very good at. Moms often like being a hostess, so you might give one of them the project of planning wedding-weekend activities for out-of-town guests. (That's my favorite activity for mothers.) Another good project is to ask mom to be in charge of hotel-welcome gift bags. Maybe your dad likes to make homemade beer or wine? If so, perhaps he can make favors for your guests.

We asked Jen's mom to be in charge of the bridal shower. She also had a lot of input on the post-wedding brunch and the weekend activities. It's empowering (and helpful to the partners!) when a parent has stuff to do and for which to feel responsible.

## Step Seven: Keep the Projects Coming

Parents like to feel that they're contributing. If your parents live out-of-state, when they come to town, distract them some more. This means that you should ask them to write out escort cards, bring gift bags to the hotel and tidy your house so that it's clean after your honeymoon. They will have nervous energy. Channel it to your own benefit.

We had Jen's mom assembling out-of-town guest gift bags and writing out escort cards. We had her parents, her sister, and her sister's boyfriend over our condo loading up the car with everything, tidying our house and taking out the trash. These "assignments" worked like a charm and everyone had fun with them.

A final thought: I know that these tips may seem manipulative or overly strategic but I promise, they really work.

## Kid-Friendly Weddings

In the last chapter, I mentioned setting policies about whom to invite to your wedding, and one of the "categories" of invitees is children. Initially, many of my clients were in their forties and fifties and had been together for many years. It's common for such couples, having waited for decades for legal recognition of their relationship, to be homeowners and to have children. When that's the case, the wedding will simply not be a Saturday night dance party with the guests doing the "Electric Slide."

In one such instance, my clients Sue and Anne were doctors, together for eleven years with three children. The wanted a festive, Sunday afternoon, interfaith family wedding—with one hundred and ten adults and seventy children! They lived in an adorable, pale-yellow house on a quiet street in a diverse Boston neighborhood and the two littlest kids (twins, a boy and a girl) were still nursing. How do you plan a wedding where there will be seventy kids? This is not your average wedding challenge, but we hit the ground running to pull this one off.

This couple and I looked at many wedding venues with large, nicely landscaped lawns. I helped them choose a venue with a large lawn and pond (providing ample space for the children to play), and to accommodate their large guest list in a tent. The floral designer created a gorgeous chuppah with a natural, curly-willow archway, and the ceremony was held near the pond. The interfaith ceremony was officiated by a rabbi and the bridal processional included the partners' children.

Later, the band performed a hora and lots of other family-friendly music. The caterer designed an entirely separate menu for the children, including a station for them during "mocktail hour." We hired a children's entertainer as well as someone to lead the children in arts and crafts throughout the afternoon. The end result was a beautiful, naturally elegant wedding with something for everyone. The guests were entertained for hours.

I've planned many weddings for gay and lesbian couples with children—or with children on the way—or where lots of children were welcome. You'll want to be sure to hire one or more babysitters who can provide toys and DVDs for the younger children, in particular. Here are some more tips for planning a family friendly wedding:

- Choose a venue that has a room where a babysitter can set up. If you can't set aside a children's room, set up a table for children's activities. This table can include crayons and coloring books, toys and puzzles. Put the babysitter (or someone else) in charge of this area.
- Communicate with your caterer about the number of children who will be attending, their approximate ages, and any needs you may have for high chairs, booster seats, cups with plastic lids and children's food (pizza, chicken fingers, grilled cheese, sliced fruit and French fries are always popular).
- Coordinate with your band or DJ to play kid-friendly songs (for example, you may want to pass on "Baby Got Back" in favor of "The Hokey Pokey"). I asked one band to play the theme song to the show *The Fairly OddParents* during the reception. The kids loved it.
- Hire children's entertainers to distract the children so the adults can play. I work with an outstanding entertainer who has a Jedi Knight Training show and a Hogwarts Academy show that is appropriate for kids under the age of ten. The shows are perfect for weddings.

There are some really creative ways to involve kids in the ceremony itself. If you do have one or more children, you can acknowledge them in your vows, or make a vow to the child/children. If you have a unity ritual, a third candle can represent the child/children. Your officiant can help you find the best way to incorporate kids into your wedding ceremony, should you choose to do so.

# Chapter 4:
# The Wedding Party

Your best man. Your best woman. Your maid of honor. Your attendant. Your groomsman. Your bridesmaid. Your person of honor. Your best person. Your best people. Your man of honor. Your bestie. Your bridesmates. Your bestmates.

Who *are* these people? Take your pick of any or none at all. This is one of those areas where I'll say "anything goes at a gay wedding." You can mix it up and have opposite-gender individuals as your attendants. You can have no attendants at all. You can "share" attendants. Why not? This is a gay wedding and you can do whatever the heck you want. I'm not going to keep saying that, I promise. But you *can*. Over half of the weddings I've planned have had no wedding parties at all—and that's perfectly wonderful because it keeps the emphasis on the couple.

That said, many couples do want a wedding party and if you do, you'll want to know what to expect from, your attendant(s). (For the purpose of being gender-neutral and for ease of communicating, I'll be relying heavily on the word "attendant." But truthfully, I've heard all sorts of variations.) Jen and I had two girls on each side, four attendants in total. All but one was actually straight. The girls were in charge of invitations and activities at the bridal shower. They also threw us a bachelorette party, but otherwise they didn't have a ton of responsibility. We asked them to wear navy but gave them complete freedom in their outfit selection. We didn't ask them to give toasts or to dance with one another.

*Our wedding party*

Here are the *traditional* roles of members of a wedding party. You'll notice they tend to have a lot of responsibility.

## Maid of Honor

- Goes dress and veil shopping with the bride.
- Throws the bridal shower if a family member does not.
- Helps assemble and mail invitations.
- Attends the wedding rehearsal.
- Has her hair and makeup done with the bride before the wedding.
- Helps the bride to dress before the wedding.
- Participates in the wedding processional.
- Holds the groom's wedding ring.
- Holds the bride's flowers.
- Helps with the bustle after the ceremony.
- Dances with the best man at the wedding reception.

# Best Man

- Throws a bachelor party.
- Helps the groom choose a tuxedo.
- Attends the wedding rehearsal.
- Helps the groom get dressed before the wedding.
- Participates in the wedding processional, or waits at the altar with the groom and officiant.
- Holds the bride's wedding ring.
- Toasts the happy couple at the wedding reception.
- Dances with the maid of honor at the wedding reception.
- Returns any rental tuxedos.

# Bridesmaids

- Attend the shower.
- Attend the wedding rehearsal.
- Participate in the wedding processional.
- Dance with groomsmen at the reception.

# Groomsmen

- Attend the bachelor party.
- Seat wedding guests.
- Attend the wedding rehearsal.
- Unroll the wedding runner, if one is used.
- Participate in the wedding processional or wait at the altar with the groom and officiant.
- Dance with bridesmaids at the wedding reception.

# Flower Girl

Typically, flower girls are young and not much is expected of them. They'll often carry a basket of flowers during the wedding processional. Sometimes they will toss petals on the aisle runner during her processional.

# Ring Bearer

The little guy serving as the ring bearer usually isn't asked to do too much. He will often walk next to the flower girl during the processional while holding the pillow with the wedding rings. If you do have a ring bearer, there's a new product that's a great alternative to the traditional ring pillow. Paloma's Nest is a company that created the Original Ring Bearer Bowl, a ceramic bowl that can have your choice of wording. It's adorable and truly an heirloom wedding item. The bowls can be purchased at www. PalomasNest.com.

*The Original Ring Bearer Bowl*

# Wedding Party Tips

Keep in mind the following as you are discussing your own wedding party:

- It's okay if someone declines your request to be in your wedding party. No one is obligated to accept—the person asked might have financial challenges, work issues or some other reason. Don't guilt anyone out.
- Choose the people with whom you are closest to be your attendant.
- You don't have to ask someone to be your attendant just because you were in his or her wedding. Stand firm if you don't want someone as your attendant. (*Not* asking someone can be an emotional landmine—but it's *your* wedding.

- You don't have to have the same number of attendants on either side. It doesn't have to be matchy-matchy. (You don't have to go out and make new best friends or invite people you'd rather not for the sake of "symmetry.") I repeat: no symmetry required.
- Some people are not comfortable with gender roles associated with wedding tasks. You might want to check this out with people you'd like to serve as your attendants.
- Someone other than the "best person" will often toast the couple at the reception.
- Many gay weddings don't have bachelor parties or bridal showers.
- Many gay couples don't ask their attendants to dance with one another.
- Many gay couples don't expect all their female attendants to wear the same dress, if they are even asked to wear a dress at all. For dresses, I'm a fan of designers like J Crew and Aria, where you can match the fabric in a variety of dresses that flatter every figure.
- There are often no formal introductions at a gay wedding, or if there are, it's typically just the newlyweds.

In short, if you're planning a gay wedding, there's a good chance you'll be asking a lot less of your attendants than your heterosexual counterparts would.

## Who Pays for What?

Your attendants are responsible for their own wedding attire, travel expenses, and accommodations. If you are *offering* an attendant an opportunity (such as access to the hair and makeup artist), your attendant can cover that cost him or herself. On the other hand, if you *require* an attendant to do anything special (like a spa day for the girls), then you as host should cover that cost.

You should buy each attendant a thank-you gift.

## The Wedding Shower

Traditionally, the mother of the bride or the maid of honor hosts a bridal shower (typically around lunchtime) for all the local ladies invited to the wedding. At the bridal shower, lots of gifts are opened, sometimes games are played, and sometimes the bride is forced to wear a funny hat made of paper plates and gift bows.

You don't have to do that.

Couples who are already settled into a home (with several cabinets full of Crate and Barrel dishes), generally don't want a wedding shower, as they probably already have everything they need. That's great. It saves everyone some money.

Couples who are just starting out are more likely to want a shower (both brides *and* grooms can have wedding showers). These are still often thrown by moms or by attendants, and some of the same traditions hold true. I hope that you don't have to wear a hat made of paper plates and bows but it is a fun and silly tradition.

Our shower was thrown by Jen's mom. The idea was to do something a little nontraditional, so knowing the two of us, she threw us a dessert and champagne shower in the middle of the afternoon. The event was held at a restaurant that specializes in decadent desserts.

Our attendants were in charge of the décor and the fun, so they created a "Bernadette and Jen trivia" game and they organized an inter-table competition. It was hilarious, and still very low-key.

To avoid creating a lot of attention, we opted for a display shower, in which the gifts are set up on display, unwrapped. Not only did we not have to be the center of attention while ooohing and ahhing over gifts, but we didn't have to wear funny hats. I know our guests enjoyed this nontraditional take on the shower because it was different and fun.

# Bachelor and Bachelorette Parties

Of course bachelor and bachelorette parties are heterosexual traditions but they're also a really good time—and another excuse for a party. Here again, couples who are more settled tend not to have these parties, while couples that are starting out often do.

Being a same-sex couple can mean that you have a joint party or two separate parties. If you have separate groups of friends, separate parties are generally the way to go. But if your friends are merged, then I like a big party.

I have two brides who are partying independently and meeting up at a club at the end of the night. Jen and I chose to party together over an informal dinner, followed by a trip to a strip club (the most tasteful one in the city, if you can believe it). We were both on our best behavior (look, don't touch) and a great time was had by all.

Some couples who party separately have a "don't ask, don't tell policy" (a "what happens in Vegas, stays in Vegas" kind of thing). If you plan on misbehaving that's not a bad plan—just don't drunk-dial or drunk-text at the end of the night. No unnecessary drama, right!

# Chapter 5:
## The Challenge in Coming Out

A wedding averages forty-three different vendors. Everyone from the hair and makeup artists, to the limo driver, to the coat-check guy. And when you as a gay couple are planning your wedding, you have to come out over and over and over again—to all of these people, both those whom you hire and those you do not. Every time you visit a venue or taste a cake, you must come out. Every time you interview a florist or a wedding planner, you must come out. This could mean coming out one hundred plus times over the course of planning your wedding. And unfortunately, in many places (about half of the U.S. states), it's legal for vendors to say, "I can't help you. I don't do gay weddings."

If your state is *not* on this list, vendors can legally discriminate against you:

| | |
|---|---|
| California* | Minnesota* |
| Colorado* | Nevada |
| Connecticut | New Hampshire |
| Delaware | New Jersey* |
| District of Columbia* | New Mexico* |
| Hawaii* | New York |
| Illinois* | Oregon* |
| Iowa* | Rhode Island* |
| Maine* | Washington* |
| Maryland | Wisconsin |
| Massachusetts | Vermont* |

**\*Transgender tip:** The states that are marked with a star include gender identity/expression in their non-discrimination policy. The states without the star do not.

Of course, every vendor my company works with is going to be great, but I know that there are other vendors that won't be as hospitable. If you are two women, when you enter a store, you will encounter vendors who will ask, "who's the bride?" even if they are gay-friendly. If you are two grooms, you will encounter vendors who will ask, "where's the bride?" even if they are gay-friendly.

I'm all about being pre-emptive and speaking up right from the beginning. If being vocal early on reduces stress later, then go for it. Here's how you should come out when speaking on the phone with a potential vendor (example if you are a groom): "hi, I'm getting married to my partner John. He proposed recently and I wanted to inquire about your venue to host our gay wedding."

A few tips:

• Be pro-active in coming out. Come out right away before vendors can make any assumptions about your sexual orientation.

- Trust your instincts. If there's any awkwardness or discomfort with whomever you are talking to, call someone else. There's another vendor who would love to work with you.
- Don't be afraid to ask the vendor about his or her experience with gay weddings.
- Don't be too quick to dismiss a vendor if he or she doesn't have any experience, but seems like a nice and supportive person. You may help a worthy vendor grow his or her business.

Note that I used the phrase "gay wedding" in the sample introductory statement. Let there be no mistake that you are having a gay wedding when communicating with vendors. Some names are gender-ambiguous. Some vendors are clueless. Be clear from the get-go. It'll save you stress later. If you are sending an e-mail message, being explicit about the fact that you're planning a gay wedding will give the vendor pause and minimize any accidental use of "bride and groom" in a canned e-mail response.

**Transgender Tip:** Coming out prior to meeting with a vendor is especially important if you are a transgender person. You don't want the person you meet with to have any misunderstandings during your in-person meeting.

I need to be honest and let you know that there's a good chance you're going to encounter some heterosexism and possibly homophobia, even if you're marrying in a state where gay marriage is legal. I want to tell you this because, even as a planner, I've seen some ugly things, even with vendors I had pre-screened:

- I was invited to do a presentation to a group of wedding professionals on how to work with gay couples, and one of the vendors in the audience blatantly told me upon my arrival that she didn't work with gay couples, and instead referred them to a colleague.

- I took two brides to meet with a florist with whom I'd previously worked and the florist said when we walked in, "so, which one of you is the bride?"
- I booked a trolley (a company I'd used before) for my grooms' wedding guests, and the man who helped me with my reservation asked me "which way do they swing?" when I told him it was a same-sex wedding.
- At another wedding, the trolley driver told me he couldn't wait to see the bride and groom. I reminded him there were two grooms. The driver rolled his eyes and blessed himself.
- The limo driver who drove my grooms was looking for a restroom while he waited for the ceremony to end. Someone suggested the basement of a nearby library. He said, "I know what happens in that basement bathroom and I guess I should watch myself around these guys."

I am not telling you these things to freak you out, to deter you from planning a fabulous wedding, or to scare you into hiring me or another gay wedding planner. Not at all. However, there's a misconception that all vendors are on board, accepting and understanding, because gay weddings have been happening in some places for several years now. I wish it were. And in the above situations, my clients didn't have to experience these situations themselves.

As you do your wedding planning homework online and start to identify vendors, you'll stumble upon a number of online gay wedding directories including:

- EnGAYgedweddings.com
- GayRites.net
- GayWeddings.com
- Gay.Weddings.com
- PurpleUnions.com

- QueerlyWed.com
- RainbowWeddingNetwork.com
- SoYoureEnGAYged.com
- UltimateGayWeddings.com

Most of these sites are "pay for play," which means that a wedding vendor can advertise on them without providing any validation or proof that they are, in fact, gay-friendly. The only directory that screens vendors to make sure that the language on their website and in their marketing materials is, in fact, inclusive, is SoYoureEnGAYged.com. The other sites will allow vendors to sign up for free listings without a thorough background check or screening process. Accordingly, I again recommend that when you call vendors, any vendor, anywhere, referred to you by anyone or any place at all, you should come out right away and make no mistake about the fact that you're planning a gay wedding.

The following chart compares Web sites that market themselves as resources to gay and lesbian couples. You can see which ones offer real wedding blogging, where you can buy a LGBT cake topper and invitations, and so forth. Be aware, however, that you might not find the information you need on these sites. There are some others that are inclusive (to gay and straight couples) but not exclusive. For a very complete wedding planning experience, with budget information, task lists, photo inspiration boards, and more, check out www.MyKPWedding.com

And for complete eye-candy, beautiful images, fun giveaways, and more check out www.WeddingChicks.com

| Web site | Vendor Directory | Vendors Pre-Screened | Planning Tools | Legal Resources | Boutique | Wedding Registry | Message Board | Real Gay Weddings | Real Gay Wedding Blogging |
|---|---|---|---|---|---|---|---|---|---|
| EnGAYgedWeddings.com | x | x | x | x | | | | | |
| GayRites.net | x | | | | x | | | | |
| GayWeddings.com | x | | x | | x | x | x | x | |
| GayWeddings.com | x | | x | | x | | | x | |
| QueerlyWed.com | x | | x | | | | x | x | |
| PurpleUnions.com | x | | | | | | | | |
| RainbowWeddingNetwork.com | x | | x | | | x | | | |
| | | | | | | | | | |
| SoYoureEnGAYged.com | x | | x | | | | | x | x |
| UltimateGayWeddings.com | x | | x | | | | x | | |
| | | | | | | | | | |
| | | | | | | | | | |

51

# Chapter 6: What to Wear

Of course, it's super-fun to pick out what you'll wear to your gay wedding. That said, the outfit-selection process can be stressful. I try to guide my clients in making good choices that reflect their taste (without providing too much of my own opinion).

## For the Ladies

I talk with a lot of brides, and one of their biggest sources of angst and frustration is the issue of what to wear at their wedding. A lot of lesbian brides don't want to wear a wedding gown (and a lot of lesbian brides would rather be called bridegrooms). I didn't.

Sometimes you have to get really creative.

Many of my clients have had custom creations or have bought off-the-rack at Banana Republic, J.Crew, Hugo Boss, Nordstrom or Bloomingdale's. I've had brides in tunics, in saris, in white dresses (not gowns), and in other colored dresses. I've had some in black suits and tuxedoes, some in white suits and tuxedoes. There's no tradition here: use your imagination and allow yourself to be inspired.

If you are interested in the trends, my analysis of about 200 lesbian couples indicated that this is what they wore:

- 46% of lesbian couples had one partner in a wedding gown or dress and one in a pants suit or tuxedo
- 42% of lesbian couples had both partners in a wedding gown or dress
- 12% of lesbian couples had both partners in a pants suit or tuxedo

*Brides each wearing white wedding dresses*

## Wedding Gown Shopping

Of course, many lesbian brides want to wear a beautiful, white wedding gown. They want the fantasy that they grew up with, the feeling, as one of my clients put it, "of being in a big room full of wedding dresses, surrounded by my friends and a bottle of champagne." Their wedding day is the day that they get to live the fairytale, be the princess.

If you are such a bride, as my wife Jen was, there's a good chance you're going to be asked questions about your groom when you go dress shopping. My best advice: when you call to make an appointment, explicitly tell the person making the appointment that yours is a lesbian wedding and that there is no groom. State that you wanted to be clear about this from the beginning. This script is an example of how easy it can be to come out to a vendor:

> Bride: Hi, I'm calling to set up an appointment for a dress consultation.
>
> Staff: Great, thanks for calling! When would you like to come in?
>
> Bride: Next Saturday
>
> Staff: How about 9:00 AM?
>
> Bride: Perfect.
>
> Bride: One more thing—I want to give you the heads-up that this is a lesbian wedding. I'm marrying a woman—there's no groom.
>
> Staff: Okay, no problem. Can I get your name and phone number to confirm the appointment?

Then, when you actually go to your appointment, if you are going with your mom or some attendants, I'd encourage you to ask them to go inside ahead of you and remind the staff that this is a lesbian wedding.

> Attendant: Hi, I'm here with my best friend for her 9:00 AM dress appointment.
>
> Staff: Great, where's the bride?
>
> Attendant: She's still outside, but I wanted to remind you that she's not marrying a man so

there's no groom. She's a lesbian bride. Can you make sure the sales assistant knows this so my friend is totally comfortable?

Staff: Of course, no problem.

I can't stress enough the importance of being transparent up front. There's nothing worse than the awkwardness that comes from a vendor trying to make up for his or her assumptions. This is a terrible situation to find yourself in, as in this scenario:

Staff: We're going to have fun dress shopping for you today! So when's the big day?

Bride: July 18

Staff: Congratulations! What's the lucky groom's name?

Bride: Her name is Sarah.

Staff: Oh, okay. {awkward pause} It's a beautiful day today, isn't it?

**Transgender Tip:** Pay attention to the script above. It will be especially important to come out over the phone and again before your appointment begins.

## Selecting a Dress

Gown or dress shopping is a very emotional process. And it's one that you should start fairly early on in your planning process. In a way, getting a dress symbolizes that the wedding is actually happening. It's a big deal for those who choose to wear dresses. So how do you choose a dress that makes you feel confident, sexy, and comfortable? How do you pick out the one garment that will represent you on the biggest day of your life?

*These brides each wore a dress in their wedding colors (brown and pink)*

*A white dress and a white suit*

What looks good on your body? Be honest with yourself. Are you petite or tall? What are your best features and what are your problem areas? Are you curvy or a beanstalk? There's truly a dress for everyone.

## Bustles and Alterations

When you go shopping, there's a good chance that your size may not be in stock. Wedding dress vendors typically carry a few sample sizes (around size 8-10) in each style and then clamp the back so you get a sense of how the dress will actually look. After that, they'll take your measurements and those will be used to create your made-to-order dress.

After the dress comes in (it may take from four to six months), alterations may still be needed (running several hundred dollars and up) so be sure to plan accordingly.

I've noticed that most of my lesbian brides who wear dresses forgo a train on the dress. That's not to say that all lesbian brides do this but just a trend I've observed. If you do have a train, a bustle will have to be added by a seamstress, so that your dress can be bustled for the reception. At the fitting where the seamstress is pinning the bustle, make sure that the bustle is high enough so you can dance at the reception! This may mean busting a few dance moves out during the fitting!

If you do have a bustle, be sure to put someone (your wedding planner or your best person) in charge of learning how to tie the bustle on your wedding day! Some bustles are snapped or hooked, but most commonly they're tied with a series of ribbons. Bustles do break, so be sure to include heavy-duty safety pins (diaper pins work well) in your wedding-day emergency kit (just in case!)

*A white dress and a black suit*

*Two white suits*

## Gown Alternatives

Lesbian brides who do not want to wear wedding gowns have a harder time. The options are just so limited. Here are some of the challenges you'll encounter if you are looking for something ready-to-wear:

- If you want to wear a white suit and your wedding is in the summer, you will have a hard time shopping for it before spring. And you might not find something right away, which brings an extra layer of wedding stress. Conversely, winter-weight white suits are scarce in the summer.

- If you want to wear a suit and *not* look like you're in something you can hang back in the closet and wear to work on Monday (that is, something that is not very *officey*), your options will be further limited. Suits with more drape to the design can be scarce!

- If you look for a men's tuxedo to rent or buy, there's a very good chance that the fit won't be right. The legs and sleeves will probably be too long and the shoulders too broad. You're going to have to find a gay-friendly tailor who will alter the heck out of that suit—but it can be done.

Truly your best bet is to approach your wedding suit the same way a woman wearing a wedding gown might approach her attire: see it as an investment. Your suit doesn't have to be something you'll wear again. It's special and it's okay if it stays in the back of your closet for eternity. If you truly want to look your sharpest, I strongly recommend that you have a suit custom made by a tailor, which can run $1000 and up. It's a lot of money, but it's worth it. The suit will be made with the finest fabrics, perfectly cut for your body. You will look your best. I highly recommend that you seek the services of someone similar in your area.

And as for me at my wedding? Well, I was lucky. Banana Republic's 2009 line of summer suits included a line in white. I scored with the brand's Martin Fit trousers in white with a matching jacket. The trousers had a great flow to them and weren't too business-like. The fabric was light and soft to the touch, with a slight sheen. I totally lucked out, but I didn't find anything until May for a July wedding. Had I waited any longer, I wouldn't have had time to have something custom-made, which was my last resort.

**Transgender Tip:** If you plan to wear a wedding dress, don't stress yourself out in advance about sizing or how your body will fit into it. If you go to a bridal shop, the dress you end up with will be custom made for your body and for your wedding. There is a dress for you! You will find it and you will look beautiful!

**Green Tip:** Hemp wedding gowns used to be hideous, but now there are many stylish options. Check out www. GetConscious.com/Gownindex.html for some ideas for your gown and bridesmaids dresses. If you're environmentally aware, you might also consider a wedding dress and bridesmaids' dresses than can be worn again. Some brides who are eco-conscious also re-purpose a dress worn by their moms. Finally, there are some beautiful organic cotton dresses available. A good resource for those is www.TheCottonBride.com.

## For the Gents

Compared to the girls, the guys have it easy when it comes to dressing for a gay wedding. Men can simply go to a Mr. Tux or Men's Wearhouse and rent a tuxedo. Another option is to go to a Brooks Brothers or a Saks for a custom-made tuxedo or suit. As a groom, you can fairly easily avoid questions about the bride and find a tux that's a good fit for you. Here's what I've seen:

- Two grooms in morning suits.
- Two groom in tuxedoes.
- Two grooms in suits.

- Two grooms in a shirt and tie.

**Transgender Tip:** Depending on your body type, you may have to have a suit custom made by a tailor or the suit you buy may need to be significantly altered for you. I highly recommend that you follow the script earlier in this chapter and come out to vendors over the phone when making appointments, and again before the appointment begins.

*Two tuxes, one with a tartan vest and bowtie*

*Neither suits nor tuxes*

*Two tuxes*

Most of my clients buy their outfits and if you do so, you can get away with suit shopping without coming out. In this case, it's likely that you won't get the same kinds of questions that a bride will get. If you'd rather not come out, you don't have to.

I'm giving you permission right here to wear a wedding dress if you want to. Remember, it's *your* wedding and you can do what you want. If you want to wear a gown and look like a beautiful princess, that's your right. Be sure to use the tips I shared earlier in this chapter when calling around to bridal salons. Come out first, before the appointment, to gauge the attitude of the shop and its staff members.

Anything goes—and while I've never sent a groom down the aisle dressed in drag, you might as well work it on the best day of your life!

# Chapter 7:
# Do You Need a Wedding Planner?

I'm biased but I think that if you can afford a wedding planner, he or she is worth the expense. If you think about all the times you have to come out when planning your wedding you'll realize how nice it would be to have someone do that for you. Part of your planner's job is to make sure every vendor you meet is as sweet as pie, not discriminatory.

Taken right from my Web site, here are my top fourteen reasons (in reverse order) that you need a wedding planner:

14. You live across the country but are looking to get married in a place where it's legal and bring a bunch of loved ones with you, and have no idea who to hire or trust in that area.

13. You're very intelligent but don't have a good sense of how to create a cohesive vision and pull together the right colors, fabrics, lights, sounds, and flowers to create a wedding that tells your story.

12. Your and your partner are both busy professionals, possibly with one or more kids, a

lot of friends, family, and hobbies, and just don't have the time to make wedding plans.

11. You realize that it's less than six months to your preferred wedding date and you have no idea where to start.

10. You have been engaged for months, still don't have a date, and are too overwhelmed to sort through the 770,000 wedding venues that showed up in Google.

9. You need someone to manage your budget and make sure you stick to it.

8. You want to be sure that the vendors you hire are reliable, trustworthy, and do beautiful work.

7. You have a vision for your wedding, but don't know how to turn your ideas into reality (and you might need help convincing your fiancé that your ideas aren't that crazy).

6. You want to avoid the mistakes you've seen at other people's weddings—poor flow to the event, not enough people dancing, the wedding ending early, bad food, cheesy DJ and more.

5. You want to save money! You love the idea of a planner who can help you receive discounts from vendors and give you tips on how to save money.

4. You don't want to be asked when you walk into a bridal, cake or floral studio, "so which one of you is the bride?" or "where's the bride?"

3. The etiquette questions are driving you mad: who to invite, what wording to use, how to deal with family issues, whether to invite kids, and more.

2. You don't want to worry on your big day. The last thing you want on your wedding day is to worry about the schedule, the flow, where to put the guestbook, if the DJ will be late, the flowers and the cake.

1. And finally, you want to *enjoy* your engagement! You want to spend the months prior to your wedding spending quality time with your fiancé, planning your honeymoon, picking out china, and otherwise daydreaming about blissful married life!

Wedding planners typically provide the following services. The price for each service may vary depending on the scope of their work and where you live.

# Full Service

Full-service wedding planning is soup-to-nuts and includes everything from finding you a venue and pro-gay vendors to sending you down the aisle (if you have an aisle, of course). Creating a day-of-wedding schedule and coordinating and being responsible for all set up and breakdown is part of this service. Full-service planning should include a customized wedding budget, timeline, and task lists. Higher-end wedding planners may also provide a virtual office for all of your wedding files.

# Partial Service

Planners providing partial service generally assume you have a venue but need help nailing down some final gay-friendly vendors, as well as all of the day-of coordination services.

# Event Designer

Event designers go beyond planning and bringing together all the vendors but also come up with concepts and themes, colors and artwork, all the things necessary to bring together a cohesive vision that meets your original and personal details. Event designers coordinate flowers, linens, lighting, furniture rentals, signature cocktails, and other elements that go into the way your wedding looks and feels.

Note: Wedding planners may or may not offer event-design services. Some wedding planners have design skills and some just don't. I'm not a design genius, for example. But I'm really good with organizational stuff. Not all planners are designers and not all designers are planners. You should also be aware that some florists provide expanded services, beyond just floral design, but can offer coordinating linens, furniture, and the like.

## Day-of Coordination

Day-of coordination may be the name of this service, but month-of coordination is usually a more accurate description. This service is provided to couples that have done all the planning themselves but want to make sure their vision is perfectly executed.

I recommend that regardless of your decision about a wedding planner, you should hire a day-of coordinator. It's his or her job to take everything you've planned and execute it flawlessly. Although my company no longer offers this individual service, we did for five years and we have it down to a science. Read below to see what a good day-of coordinator does and make sure that any coordinator you hire provides these services:

- If he or she isn't familiar with the venue, the coordinator should schedule a meeting there. This helps to provide a way to get a grasp on your overall wedding vision.
- My company asks the couple five pages of questions, such as "where do you want the flowers to be moved to after the ceremony?" and "would you like special personal touches in the restrooms?" Basically, we ask questions about details that most people would never think about. Make sure that your coordinator

has a similar questionnaire and that you all sit down together to answer these questions!

- After meeting with you, your day-of coordinator should put together a day-of-wedding schedule, which is very detailed. The schedule should outline the timing for formal photos and toasts, describe movement and flow, and have set up and breakdown tasks. We send this to clients with all of the outstanding decisions highlighted, and the highlighted items are to be resolved before your wedding day. We also send the final schedule to the clients' vendors. The schedule you see should include a packing list and list of final payments due, plus tip amounts. Ensure that this is part of your coordination package!

- Your day-of coordinator should also rehearse your wedding ceremony with you. We insist on doing this with our clients so everyone can relax on their actual wedding day. And then, on your wedding day, we generally arrive two hours early for set up and decoration tasks. We now even have those fancy "Secret Service earpieces" so we can easily communicate with each other. On your wedding day, we're in charge. We manage flow, bring you champagne after your ceremony recessional, cue toasts, cue the photographer and the DJ or band for announcements, pin corsages, line up groups for formal photos, load up your car with gifts and leftover wedding cake, and generally make sure you are as relaxed as you can possibly be.

Note: If you decide you want to hire a day-of-wedding coordinator, please don't send him or her into a poorly planned wedding. Every wedding planner has a nightmare story of a day-of coordination couple that planned themselves a "hot mess" of a wedding where there were some major details missed. It's your day-of coordinator's role to alleviate stress, but not to fix your poor plans.

## Choosing a Wedding Planner

First of all, you should know that not many wedding planners have experience with same-sex weddings. Most don't. That's okay as long as: a) you're okay with it and b) your wedding planner is open minded and eager to help you. With that in mind, remember these simple things:

1. The planner must make you feel important. A planner's job is to be focused on the couple that he or she is with in the present, not the couple getting married two days later. You must be comfortable with your planner and you must be made to feel special. If the planner does his or her job right, you're going to miss that person after the wedding because it was like you became old friends. And if you're unsure about whether you and your wedding is a priority, speak up immediately!

2. Trust is critical. You have to trust your planner with your vision but also with your heart. The reality is that your planner is entrusted to come out for you and to connect you with the right vendors for the job—vendors who you, in turn, can trust. You don't want anyone with issues of homophobia or heterosexism on your wedding day.

3. Your wedding is your wedding—that's why I'm okay with bride and groom-zillas. You're the boss and your wedding shouldn't feel cookie-cutter to you. Your planner should understand your vision fully and is the individual who will bring that vision to life. He or she acts as your representative to vendors and even in some cases, to family or wedding party members.

4. Your planner must be organized. It sounds like a no-brainer, but your planner must step up and have an organized plan for your wedding. Paperwork and contracts must all go through you. All decisions must be confirmed with you. You should be able to see your budget at all times. Your planner should never be late for meetings. You have to trust your planner with the little details.

5. Your planner should be crafty and creative. Well, not necessarily crafty – I'm admittedly not a master of the DIY. In any event, your planner should take your ideas, bring his or her own, and create a cohesive theme. Planners should have resources— books and magazines and blog links to show you. They should provide you with color palates and design ideas.

## About Using Your Friends

Your friends are guests at your wedding. Guests! They should be treated like guests! They will probably be giving you a gift. They'll probably be giving you emotional support through your stressful months of planning! No matter how bridezilla or groomzilla you get, no matter how crafty and do-it-yourself you are, and no matter how low your budget, your friends should not be working **at** your wedding.

That means: no moving of chairs, no post-wedding cleanup or breakdown, no food or bar service, no pseudo-professional photography, no gathering of groups for formal photos, and no DJing.

The following list is a great guideline for how to utilize the assistance of your friends:

- To officiate your wedding ceremony.
- To sing or perform music at your wedding ceremony.
- To make announcements (as long as there aren't too many announcements, and as long as only one friend is in charge).
- To make your wedding cake (prior to the wedding day).
- To drop off setup and décor materials.
- To provide some set up assistance (only if you don't have a wedding planner, and only if those friends are not in the wedding party).

- To videotape the event (only if you have a friend who really enjoys being behind the camera—we all have one of those).

Remember, in most cases, your friends aren't professionals. If the video or the cake, for example, doesn't come out perfectly, you can't resent them for it. If they are in charge of wedding setup and they oversleep, have a family emergency, or a flat tire, you can't blame them—you're not paying them.

# Chapter 8:
# Choosing a Venue

What kind of wedding do you want to have?

Most of us have been to many straight weddings before the laws began to change and allowed us to have our own gay weddings. So now that you can have your own gay or lesbian wedding, what kind of wedding do you want?

I was raised as a Catholic, and all of the weddings I'd been to prior to 2004 featured a ceremony and Mass in a Catholic Church (usually in the New York metropolitan area).

What kind of wedding do you want? There are lots of choices. When I meet with clients, once I've established their projected guest-count and budget, I usually start thinking about their wedding by breaking it down like a game. As a couple answers the questions, my mind narrows down the options as if the event was a *Choose Your Own Adventure* book. Once the questions are answered, I always have a short list of venues in my head. To start creating the type of wedding you want, here are some questions that you and your partner should be asking yourselves:

1. Do you want a Saturday night dance party-type of event or a Sunday, elegant brunchy type of event? A daytime or a nighttime wedding?

2. Do you want to have the ceremony in the same location as the reception?
3. Do you want to have access to an outdoor area?
4. Do you have a lot of friends and family traveling from out of state?
5. Do you have a lot of big partiers/drinkers on your guest list?
6. Is your style:
   a) urban/contemporary,
   b) industrial/loft-like,
   c) country/rustic,
   d) historic/classically elegant,
   e) casual/beachy?
7. Do you require a view of some sort?
8. Are you planning to feed everyone a full meal or would you rather have a cocktail-party type atmosphere the whole time?

Asking yourselves these questions will quickly narrow the list of potential sites. As a wedding planner, it's my job to ask questions like this when I first meet a couple. You can cut out all the photos you want from wedding magazines and bridal blogs, but you're ultimately going to want a wedding that reflects your personality and your culture, your sense of humor and your sense of style—not someone else's.

*A rustic wedding venue*

You'll soon discover that venues come in the following general categories, so when venue shopping, be sure to look at these categories as possible host sites. You may be able to cross some of these types of spaces off the list right away, or be drawn to a particular type of space:

- Halls (including Elks Club, Knights of Columbus, and the like).
- Hotels, resorts and inns (the Kimpton chain is the most gay-friendly of the lot).
- Historic spaces (including old mansions, municipal buildings, libraries, historic homes, and so forth).
- Museums (art museums, industry museums, technology, science, and so forth).
- Colleges and universities.
- Clubs (country clubs, golf clubs, and yacht clubs).
- Restaurants
- Function spaces (a catch-all which may include conference centers, retreats, banquet halls, wedding halls, wineries and others).

The right category of space is the first step in the venue selection process. The right venue can reflect your wedding vision without necessarily needing to be dressed up a whole lot.

When you book a venue, in most cases, you'll receive the space for eight hours, which means a five-hour wedding. That leaves three hours—two for setup and one for breakdown, which is the industry standard. If your ceremony is in the same place as the reception, that usually cuts into the five hour rental time unless you pay for an additional thirty- to sixty-minute rental.

Please plan accordingly when you think through your wedding decoration and setup projects. You have a limited time in which to work and some venues won't let you drop off items prior to your wedding day.

One of the first steps in planning (after you set your budget and guest list) is to go venue shopping. I highly recommend you go venue shopping with *no set wedding date in mind*. Finding a place to get married is one of the most stressful parts of planning—it's such a big deal, really—especially if the venue also provides the food and drink, another really big deal! And in many areas, there are tons of choices, which makes coming up with a short list fairly overwhelming.

When you go venue shopping, I highly recommend that you check out about five to six places in one day. I call these *marathon site visits*. Each venue will be fresh in your mind as you compare them and the cream of the crop will stick out in your mind. As you're shopping, find out the answers to the following questions:

- If applicable, have any gay weddings been performed at the site? Is there a policy of acceptance throughout their entire staff, not just the member of the sales team who is trying to get your money, but also the server who will give you your dinner?*
- If applicable, how many overnight guest rooms are available for guests? Are there any minimum nights' stay requirements? Is a discount available on large blocks of rooms?
- Ensure there are two plus rooms/spaces you'll have access to, or, if it's one large room, that it can be partitioned or screened. One space will be for the ceremony/dinner and the second for the cocktail hour.
- Is there plenty of space inside for a ceremony if the weather is poor, which can then be turned over for a reception while the guests go somewhere else during cocktail hour?
- Where is cocktail hour held?

- Is there space for a band or DJ? Are there plenty of electrical outlets?
- What is the fee for the space? Is the fee waived with a food and beverage minimum? Is the fee waived with guest room bookings?
- Is there an additional fee for an onsite ceremony? If so, does that extra fee get you an extra hour of rental time (six hours instead of five), or does an onsite ceremony cut into your five-hour rental time?
- Is there a "holding area" where you can get ready before the ceremony, or wait before the processional?
- What other fees are there? Do they charge for bartenders and cake cutting?
- Do they add gratuity and administrative charges to the bill?
- Can all of your guests fit in one function room or do you have to use adjoining side rooms?
- Does the venue provide tables and chairs or do they need to be rented? What size tables and what kinds of chairs do they own?
- Does the venue provide a dance floor or does that need to be rented?
- Can you choose your own wine or must you select wine from a limited list?
- What do the grounds look like during the season of your wedding?
- Is the function space available only during a certain time of day or during certain months of the year? This may sound peculiar, all sorts of restrictions can be placed on a space's availability. For example, many spaces in Provincetown, Massachusetts are not available in July and August because of peak tourist traffic and some places like museums won't allow daytime weddings because they are open for business.

- Does the event need to end at a particular time? Where will the guests who want an after party go?
- What are the overtime charges for events that run long?
- Does the venue host more than one wedding in a day?
- If there are two weddings in two different parts of the venue on the same day, will there be noise overlap or will guests run into one another?
- Is there a staff member who will be available during the event for any questions?
- Any there restrictions (including local ordinances) on candles, rose petals, rice, confetti, or anything else? For example, some places require a fire marshal if candles will be lit.
- Does the venue require the use of certain vendors? For example, some venues require you use a certain bakery for a wedding cake.
- For an outdoor wedding, is there typically a problem with mosquitoes during certain times of year? Do they spray the grounds?
- Is there plenty of parking for all your guests? Is it complimentary? Is there valet parking?
- Does the facility have central heat and/or air-conditioning?
- How many restrooms are on the premises?
- Does the venue have liability insurance? Do they require that vendors carry it also?
- Is there ample power for all of your décor needs? For example, lighting can use a lot of power. Do they provide extension cords? How are cords made inconspicuous?
- What's the lighting like during the time of day you plan to marry? The answer to this may inform whether you need to bring in a lighting designer.

- What does the venue provide in terms of décor? Do they provide votives on each table?
- What do their chairs, flatware, glassware, china, and linens look like? Do their house linens drape all the way to the floor? (You don't want to see the legs of the table.)
- Is there a coat check? Is there a fee for it? If so, can is it hosted?
- How much time prior to and after the wedding is available for setup and breakdown? Does the venue staff help with that? What services does their wedding or event coordinator provide? Does he or she help with setting up all of your personal details or touches? Will that person confirm your other vendors and send them a schedule? Will he or she line up the wedding party and send you down the aisle? Note: most venues don't provide these services, but if they do, you may be able to avoid hiring a day-of coordinator.
- Is it possible to have the wedding rehearsal onsite the day prior to your wedding day (assuming the ceremony is onsite)?
- Is it possible to drop off decorations the day or week prior to the wedding?
- Is there a sound system that an iPOD or CDs can be plugged into? (This is in the event that you don't take my advice not to use an iPOD).
- Is the venue financially solvent? This may sound like a ridiculous question but I know of several wedding venues that closed during the economic crisis of 2009, leaving couples high and dry, in some cases with less than a month before the wedding date.

*Transgender tip: This is especially true with a transgender bride or groom

Green tip: There are many hotels and other venues that are energy-efficient, use environmentally friendly products, have comprehensive recycling programs, and minimize water, waste, and toxins. Other spaces charge a rental fee that supports efforts to preserve beautiful places. When you're looking to be green, consider these spaces first!

Once you choose a venue, you'll be working closely with them throughout the process. It's very important to feel comfortable with the venue you choose, especially if they are also providing food and beverages. They will be receiving the bulk of your wedding budget and I just want you to be happy.

## Using a Private Residence

In theory, there are some nice advantages to planning a wedding at your home or another private residence. The home could have a special meaning to you. You could save on a venue rental fee. You are not limited by an eight-hour rental period and can set up and break down at your leisure. The party could go all night if you want.

But don't be blinded by the advantages and think through these potential obstacles before making your final decision:

- How is your septic system? Can it handle fifty or more guests? Do you have two or more restrooms that guests can use? Will you have to rent portapotties or a luxury portatpotty trailer?
- How is your parking situation? Is there enough parking for all of the vendors in the driveway? What about the guests? Will you have to hire a valet or rent a lot and provide shuttle service?
- Is the home big enough for everyone to be inside for dinner and dancing? or will you require a tent? Are you prepared to deal with the damage that tents (and the tent delivery truck) cause to the lawn?
- Is there a good spot on the property for a wedding ceremony? What if it rains?

- Are there any noise ordinances in the city or town where the wedding would be held?
- Are there nosey neighbors or neighbors who would call the police to complain about noise?
- Is there a large kitchen onsite? The caterer will have a lot of food to warm up or prepare and will need plenty of counter space and ovens. If you can't offer that, the caterer may have to set up a catering tent or you may have to rent convection ovens.
- How many amps of electricity does the home have? Are there some circuits with available power? If you are bringing in a tent, the lighting and heating of the tent requires significant power. If you are bringing in a DJ or band, they require significant power. So does a nice portapotty. Find out if you have enough electrical power to support the event or whether you will need to rent a generator.
- Is the home in an area known to have poor drainage in the event or rain? Is it especially buggy in the summer and if so, can the property be sprayed?

In general, unless it's a very well-equipped property or your wedding has fewer than fifty guests, I advise against holding a wedding in someone's home or on their property. The logistics can get very complicated and if you decide to go this route, I would definitely suggest that you hire a wedding planner to make sure that all of these details are covered.

Please use a caterer for your wedding in a private residence. Don't rely on your friends, family, or let alone, yourself, to prepare food. If you need to, you can prepare the food in advance and rent waitstaff and bartenders to serve it, but please outsource at least some of this for your own sanity!

# Outdoor Weddings

Now, I know that I live and work mostly in New England, so I have a bias. We don't have sunshine every day like they do in Los Angeles, so we always always always have to have a rain plan for weddings. We have our beautiful coastline and many people love beachy weddings, but there has to be a rain plan, and unfortunately sometimes that rain plan doesn't have the same appeal as the outdoor affair.

If you find yourself in a situation where your perfectly planned outdoor wedding gets rained out and you're forced inside, think about asking your photographer to do another shoot of you and your partner (kind of like an engagement shoot) in your wedding wardrobe on another day when it's beautiful outside.

Things to think about when planning an outdoor wedding:

- Is a tent required or is there enough room inside if the weather is poor?
- How cold does the area get in the evening? Will heaters be required inside the tent?
- How warm does the area get in the evening? Will air conditioners or fans be required inside the tent?
- Do the grounds get buggy during certain seasons?
- Are there any drainage issues that could make for excess mud?
- How far do the guests have to walk to get to the restrooms?
- Is there plenty of space inside for a ceremony if the weather is poor, and can it then be turned over for a reception while the guests go somewhere else during cocktail hour?
- Is there adequate lighting on the property in the evening?
- Are there any eyesores that may need to be covered up or screened off?

- Is there any foot traffic that may pass through the area or is there security to ensure that your space is completely private?

## Tents and Dance Floors

If you do have to rent a tent, you should book one as soon as you find the venue. Keep in mind that you'll also have to rent a dance floor.

There are a few major variables, such as your guest count and the type of dinner you are having (cocktail reception, buffet or food stations, or seated dinner), but in general, the following applies:

- For a wedding with round dinner tables and room for dancing, you'll want a tent that includes enough space for approximately 18 square feet per person.
- If you are having a DJ, add 200 square feet.
- If you are having a band, add 300 square feet.

- If you are having a buffet or food stations, add 100 square feet for every fifty guests.
- If you are having a bar, add 50 square feet per bar.

Using this math, based on a one hundred-person wedding with a sit-down dinner (not a buffet) and two bars, you will be looking at 2100 square foot tent (approximately). If you have to choose between a slightly smaller tent or a slightly bigger tent, bigger is better!

Tents come in all shapes and sizes. Some tents have poles down the middle (these are called pole tents). Some tents have poles just at the perimeter (these are called frame tents). The tent rental company will be able to give you suggestions on the right size and type of tent for your wedding, based on your unique specifications.

You will also have to rent lights for inside the tent. The tent company should provide you with some options, which may include lanterns, paper lanterns, small white bulbs around the perimeter, larger white bulbs around the perimeter, or more.

You should also plan on renting sides for the tent. These can always be quickly removed but should be rented in the event of bad weather, excess cold, or excess heat.

The tent company will also offer heaters and air conditioners, which may be necessary depending on where you live.

# Chapter 9:
# Plan On! Hotel Rooms, Wedding Web site, Save the Dates

Once you've booked your wedding venue, the next steps are to:

- Set aside hotel room blocks for out-of-town guests
- Create a wedding Web site
- Send out save-the-date cards

## Booking Hotels

I plan a lot of destination weddings, in which guests travel to a place where gay marriage is legal. I like to encourage couples to block rooms in areas where their traveling guests have activities nearby. Typically, a hotel will offers some kind of discount for your guests when you book a block of more than five rooms per night.

Keep in mind that your guests will only be at your wedding for five to six hours but may be in the city or town for a full weekend. Are there some interesting restaurants or tourist hot spots near your wedding venue? Are there places to visit near a hotel you have in mind? Even better! It's better to block rooms closer to fun activities than it is to block rooms near the wedding.

If you can set up transportation to and from the wedding from the main hotel, that's even better for your guests, who won't have to worry about drinking and driving.

I often tell my clients to block rooms at two different hotels, at two different price points. Some of their guests will want something that's very basic like a Hampton Inn, while others prefer a four- or five-star property. You should provide your guests with the hotel name(s), the quoted rate, the rate's expiration date, and instructions on booking. This information should appear on your wedding Web site and in a logistics insert that's enclosed with your wedding invitation.

When you call a hotel to inquire on a wedding room-block, ask for the group sales department. You'll then get asked a bunch of questions, probably starting with the name of the bride and groom. Overlook that question and come out right away to the person with whom you're speaking. You'll be asked about your wedding date, guest count and venue, and the dates for which you'll want to reserve guest rooms. There's a good chance the person will have to call you back with a rate, as opposed to just telling you over the phone. The discount you're offered will increase as you block a greater number of rooms.

Generally, if you are blocking fewer than fifteen rooms, the hotel will offer you an "off-the-hook rate." That's my own term, by the way, not a wedding industry term. The off-the-hook rate means that you are not under any obligation to sell all of the guest rooms you've put aside. One month prior to the wedding, unbooked rooms will be returned to hotel inventory and any wedding guests who call after that date may or may not receive the discounted rate. This is determined on a case-by-case basis, depending on availability. You may be required to sign a contract for off-the-hook rates but will not be asked for a credit card.

If your wedding requires that you set aside more than fifteen rooms, you are generally required to be "on-the-hook" for room sales. This means that you will be asked to provide a credit card in the event that 80 percent (as an example—the actual percentage will vary) of the rooms are unsold. If your guests only book 50 percent of the required number of rooms, you'll be responsible for the difference in price between the 50 percent booked and 80 percent guaranteed. Not fun. My advice is to read the contract language carefully if you need more than fifteen rooms.

## Wedding Web Sites

Many of my clients have many guests from other states at their wedding. I always recommend creating a wedding Web site as a central location for all of your wedding information, and I have some special tips to share to do this most effectively:

- Buy your personal domain (for example, www. bobandbill.com) through <u>GoDaddy.com</u> (my preferred site for domain registration).
- Set up a free wedding Web site through a site like <u>WeddingWire.com</u>, which has some nice templates for this purpose.
- Go to the "Manage My Domains" section on GoDaddy and set the personal domain to forward to the often-lengthy URL provided by WeddingWire or your other wedding website.
- Share your personal domain (e.g., www.bobandbill. com) on your save-the dates and other wedding materials.
- Use GoDaddy after the wedding when the professional photographs are ready, and change the forwarding destination of the personal domain to the link provided by your photographer.
- Tell your guests to go to your personal domain to view your professional wedding photos.

## Save-the-Dates

Once you have your venue chosen, date set, guest hotel booked and wedding Web site made, get busy on the save-the-date notices.

At this point, you may have determined a theme for your wedding and the notices can be the first item that reflects your thematic decision. Keep an eye on the big picture as you create these cards. If at all possible, indicate the URL of your wedding Web site right on the card.

The save-the-dates are the first correspondence most people will have from you about your wedding. You can send these out up to a year in advance. This way your guests can make their own travel plans (if applicable) and make arrangements to take off from work, if they need to.

While it's nice to have the save-the-date be part of the cohesive stationery design, you can be completely whimsical if you prefer. I had a couple choose a save-the-date that looked like a flyer for a country music show because they met in Nashville. I had others choose a vintage postcard style.

Here are some examples of save-the-date cards from Outvite. com:

Save the Date!

MARIO AND STEVEN
WILL BE MARRIED IN PARIS
ON JANUARY TENTH

INVITATION TO FOLLOW

PAR AVION

# Chapter 10:
# Lawfully Wedded

If you ask me, the most important part of a wedding is the "I Dos." They are, after all, what the whole day is about. A marriage is a big deal, or it should be. Gay marriages are rare and are an even bigger deal. As of 2010, gay marriage is legal only in Washington, D.C., five U.S. states and ten countries in the whole world. For that reason, I am a big fan of meaningful and personal wedding ceremonies. They don't have to be what you're used to.

You've probably been to at least one wedding with a snooze-worthy officiant and you've probably heard the same boring homily or speech over and over again. Many officiants are cheesy, but yours does not have to be. When hiring an officiant, make sure he or she has experience with gay couples or is comfortable with your marriage. Don't be afraid to check references or ask for audio or video recordings of a ceremony officiated by him or her.

Let's talk about your options:

## Guest Officiant

Many states will authorize a specific person to perform marriages on a specific date. There is typically a nominal fee and some light paperwork required for the privilege. It often takes sixty ore more days to process the application.

In many states, a loved one can get a "day pass" to officiate your wedding ceremony. There's some paperwork and a fee but it is perfectly legal and is a great way to personalize your wedding One of my favorite wedding ceremonies was officiated by an out-of-state friend of the couple. She came very prepared and worked with me to make sure the rehearsal and ceremony went smoothly. She was clear, articulate, humorous, and perfectly reverent.

Here are some tips if you are using a loved one as your guest officiant:

- Make sure you choose someone who is comfortable speaking in front of a large group.
- The guest officiant should be prepared to take on all the responsibilities of a professional officiant, including coordinating with the musicians and ceremony venue and running the wedding rehearsal.
- Be sure to make arrangements for a sound system. I always recommend a sound system with more than seventy-five guests and this is something often provided by a professional officiant. If your loved one is officiating, make sure to rent the proper equipment so he or she can be heard.
- Warn your guest officiant that this isn't a toast and that they should keep it clean, not tell inappropriate stories, and otherwise be appropriate and well behaved.
- Ask your guest officiant to speak *slowly*. Guest officiants have a tendency to get nervous and speed through a marriage ceremony. Remind the officiant to take his or time and speak slowly, not at a hurried pace.
- If you're worried about any of this, hire a professional!

## Justice of the Peace

A justice of the peace (a JP) is an officer of the state legally allowed to officiate weddings in some – but not all - states. The rules vary from state to state but in states that have a policy against discrimination on the basis of sexual orientation, a JP may not legally discriminate against you. (Nonetheless, a JP may try to avoid performing your ceremony by saying, for example, that he or she is booked for your requested date.) A JP often has some sample ceremonies and vows, and will present them as options to a couple. Some JPs will offer a custom ceremony-writing option, while others will not. Many JPs will not attend the wedding rehearsal. The average fee charged by a justice of the peace is from one hundred to two hundred dollars.

## Judge

In some states, judges are authorized to officiate marriages, in other states they're not. As with JPs, some judges will provide a couple with sample ceremonies and vows, and some will prepare a customized ceremony. Many judges will not rehearse the ceremony with the couple.

## City Clerk

A city or county clerk is authorized to marry individuals. These weddings are usually quick and as a rule, the clerk will not have met the couple before the ceremony. In these cases, there is no custom-written ceremony, no rehearsal, and nothing religious about the ceremony.

## Celebrant

You might want to hire a trained celebrant to perform your ceremony. Celebrants USA is an institute that intensely trains individuals to write and create meaningful and personal ceremonies for weddings and other major life events. Graduates are authorized to officiate marriage ceremonies and these ceremonies are custom written. Celebrants attend and run the wedding rehearsal and may or may not use religious traditions, depending on your preference. Celebrants are authorized to officiate weddings *technically* as members of the clergy but they weddings are not innately religious – unless you want them to be.

## Member of the Clergy

Clergy members include rabbis, priests, reverends, ministers, and others affiliated with a place of worship who are authorized to officiate weddings. Ceremonies performed by clergy members will most certainly have a religious slant, regardless of whether they're held in a place of worship. In many cases, the clergy member requires the couple to undergo pre-wedding counseling and sometimes he or she will require the couple to join the church if they are not already members.

## Comparing Officiants

| Type of Officiant | Legality of Ceremony | Personalized Ceremonies | Require pre-marital counseling | Rehearse Wedding | Religious Ceremony |
|---|---|---|---|---|---|
| Friend with a permit to perform a wedding | Yes, some states will allow an individual to apply for permission to officiate your wedding | Yes | No | Sometimes but a coordinator is recommended | Not usually |
| Justice of the Peace | Yes | May charge extra for this if they offer the service at all. Most provide templates for you to select from. | No | Sometimes, but a coordinator is recommended | Not usually |

| Judge | Depends on the state, some states require an extra permit | Possibly | No | Sometimes, but a coordinator is recommended | Not usually |
|---|---|---|---|---|---|
| City Clerk | Yes | No | No | No | Not usually |
| Celebrant | Yes | Yes, this a key feature of the service provided. | No | Yes | Yes |
| Member of the Clergy | Yes | Will often personalize a set script. | Usually | Yes | Yes |

# Narrowing Your Choices

To help you find the person who is best for your needs, here are some questions to ask when meeting with officiants:

- What is your experience with marriage ceremonies for same-sex couples?
- How do you charge? (You'll notice that some officiants charge a fee and others accept donations or honorariums, which often go toward the house of worship that they're affiliated with. Most often these fees are paid in advance, but if not, the payment should include a note of appreciation. This is traditionally presented by the best man, but in gay weddings, can be presented by your wedding planner, best person, or even yourself.)
- Do you provide a ceremony microphone for yourself and readers? (I recommend a microphone for weddings with more than seventy five guests if indoors, or fifty guests, if held outdoors.)
- Will you attend and run the ceremony rehearsal? If the officiant performs several ceremonies in one weekend,

find out whether he or she will be at your rehearsal. Some may not, and if you and/or your planner are not comfortable with that, choose someone else.

- Do you write custom ceremonies?
- Do you require pre-marital counseling?
- Can we write our own vows?
- Do you have sample readings?
- How long do your marriage ceremonies usually last?
- Do you have any audio or video footage of a ceremony you officiated?

Note that it's traditional for the officiant and his or her spouse (if applicable) to be invited to the rehearsal dinner and wedding. The officiants I know usually decline because they have their own families and perform at many weddings. But it is a nice gesture to invite them nonetheless.

# Chapter 11:
# From Trends to Traditions: The Gay Wedding Ceremony

My favorite part of a gay wedding is the wedding ceremony. Every gay wedding makes history. Less than 10 percent of the population is gay, and about half marry. Gay weddings are rare, historical and beautiful! You might as well make yours perfectly reflect who you are as a couple.

## Initial Considerations

There are some specific considerations that will apply to whatever type of ceremony you're planning.

Are you going to see each other before the wedding ceremony? My advice is to do so. It'll make the day go a lot more smoothly. You can get your formal photos done in advance and enjoy cocktail hour. You can relax with each other and you can even have your romantic and photographic "first look" before the ceremony. I'm all for getting dressed and doing hair and makeup (if applicable) separately, but I suggest to my clients that they meet up with each other about an hour before the ceremony.

I can't deny that there is that wonderful moment in a straight wedding when a groom sees his bride for the first time as she walks down the aisle, and I've had some brides reproduce this event. It is lovely and sometimes there are tears. But practically speaking, if you miss cocktail hour because you're too busy posing for stiff formal photos, the most important day of your life is going to go by even faster than it otherwise will (and trust me, it goes by in a flash).

How non-traditional do you want to be? Many couples I've seen choose a non-traditional ceremony because they see this as an opportunity to place their own personal stamp on it—or because they want to adhere to new gay-wedding traditions. On the other hand, some couples feel more comfortable with a ceremony that is similar to what they grew up with.

Are you having a more formal or less formal ceremony? The ceremony's formality will have an impact on the music you choose, the way you proceed down the aisle or aisles and your overall guest experience. Informal ceremonies often mean that most of your guests (except for immediate family and grandparents) are standing for the duration of the ceremony.

Are you having a religious or spiritual ceremony? Are there any spiritual, religious, or cultural rituals you want to adhere to? If you are, then your wedding may be officiated by a minister, rabbi or celebrant.

Are you having your ceremony in a place of worship? Depending on the place, the venue may have a central aisle, thereby limiting your processional options. I'll discuss place of worship options in greater detail below.

If not in a house of worship, where will the ceremony be? Does your reception venue have a good space that is ceremony worthy? Can the ceremony be in front of a fireplace, mantel, nice bookcase, or even a beautiful staircase? If so, you can get away without a great deal of floral arrangements. Would the ceremony be outside? How will you designate the ceremony space? Do you imagine a wedding arch, an arbor, a chuppah, or something else? It's important to frame the ceremony space.

How long do you want the ceremony to last? Do you truly want to be in-and-out? Is the reception more important to you than the ceremony? Are you uncomfortable being the center of attention? If these items are concerns for you, you'll probably want to plan on a very short ceremony. In my experience, informal gay wedding ceremonies tend to be fewer than ten minutes long, with more formal ceremonies lasting for twenty to thirty minutes.

What kind of music do you want to hear as you process and recess down the aisle(s)? Do you want an organist, or a DJ or band playing your favorite contemporary song? Would you like a trio of strings playing something traditional? Perhaps you have one or more very musically inclined guests who can perform ceremony music. Many of my clients choose a contemporary pop song that is played either by a few members of the band, or by the DJ.

How many attendants are you having? Keep the size of your wedding party in mind when considering where your ceremony will be held. If it's at a place of worship, a larger wedding party should fit comfortably. If it's in a less traditional venue, or the same place you're having your reception, there may be size constraints.

Do you want to enter the ceremony together or separately? Does either partner want to be the center of attention, or feel like the "bride"? I've planned only one wedding in which the two partners did not enter at the same time or together. In that instance, one of the lesbian brides waited in the ceremony area for the other to process down the aisle. In most cases, the couple walks in together or enters at the same time from two separate directions.

Are you interested in being escorted by parents or family members? At our wedding, Jen was escorted by her parents and I was escorted by my brothers (my parents had passed). Do you want to be escorted by anyone at all?

Do you want there to be a seating area designated for each side of the family? Traditionally, one side of the aisle is for the bride's family and guests, and the other side is for the groom's.

Gay weddings usually skip this tradition, but that doesn't mean that you have to. If you would like to seat guests in this manner, you should plan on having ushers.

Do you want ushers? Ushers are most often used when there's a bride's side and a groom's side! Most gay weddings do not have ushers escort guests, and many don't have ushers at all, unless they are asked to distribute ceremony programs.

Have your guests been to gay weddings before? If most of your guests have not attended a gay wedding and if they may be a little nervous or on edge, you may consider having sparkling water and wine passed before the ceremony. Offering beverages before the ceremony happens so frequently that it's become a gay-wedding tradition. It's a nice way to let your guests know that this is not your ordinary wedding—plus it takes the edge off!

Do you want to sign a sacred marriage document? In Jewish tradition, the couple signs a Ketubah before the ceremony. Quaker couples sign the Marriage Certificate. In gay weddings, the couple signs the Foundation Covenant. This is a very nice memento of your wedding day.

Do you want to have a unity ritual? The traditional unity ritual features a unity candle, which is lit by two smaller candles. The primary candle symbolizes the two families coming together. Other unity rituals include a wine ceremony and a sand ceremony, all symbolizing two becoming one. In each case there are two different kinds of wine or sand placed together in the same vessel.

Are there guests who may have difficulty standing for a long period of time? Obviously, if standing for a long time is a challenge for your guests, you may want to have a more formal ceremony or be sure to provide seating for these individuals if you're having a very informal ceremony where most of the guests stand.

## The Structure of a Traditional Gay Wedding

There comes a time, and it may be just about now—six years after the first same-sex marriages come to pass in the United

States—when we take stock of gay-wedding trends. At this point, we're starting to see some trends as gay-wedding traditions.

Now, when I'm asked by a reporter, a prospective client, a curious acquaintance, or a stranger at a cocktail party, "what's the difference between a straight wedding and a gay wedding?" my response begins with, "well, traditionally, at a gay wedding ..."

Some gay-wedding traditions follow.

**Pre-Ceremony Champagne.** There's a strong and palpable feeling of triumph and celebration at gay weddings. But before that feeling actually sets in, many of the guests (particularly those who have never before attended a gay wedding) simply don't know what to expect. So the guests start out with a great deal of anticipation; they're a little nervous, excited, and curious. We like to help them relax and so we recommend greeting them before the ceremony with champagne and sparkling water. The refreshments may be served for five to thirty minutes before the ceremony begins, and they set the tone of something a little bit different, but definitely celebratory and fun.

**The Unique Processional.** Many couples choose not to enter down one central aisle. Often the partners walk in from two different directions, each accompanied by his or her family and/ or wedding party, and the two meet in the middle.

**The Ceremony Music.** At gay weddings, pop songs are often featured. Sometimes the piece is played live and sometimes couples have the recorded version of the song played. Here are some common options:

- "All You Need is Love" by the Beatles
- "Ribbon in the Sky" by Stevie Wonder
- "Wedding Bell Blues" by Laura Nyro
- "Your Precious Love" by Marvin Gaye and Tammi Terrell
- "You Are the Sunshine of My Life" by Stevie Wonder
- "The Rainbow Connection" by Kermit the Frog

**The Validation and Affirmation.** Following the processional, the guests remain standing, champagne in hand, for the opening remarks and tradition of "validation and affirmation," which is essentially a brief introductory blessing/toast. Then the guests sit and the ceremony proceeds as you might expect, but with often a bit more emphasis on the history of the couple.

**The Foundation Covenant.** Later in the ceremony, after the vows are exchanged, the officiant asks the couple to sign the Foundation Covenant. This document is inspired by the Ketubah, Quaker wedding certificate and other sacred documents, and is an art piece signed by the couple and later by the guests. I work with one designer who creates Foundation Covenants that tie into my client's custom wedding stationery. But Foundation Covenants are also sold through the website www.ModernKetubah.com. The designer, Daniel Sroka, creates beautiful fine art pieces inspired by nature.

**The Recessional.** After the ceremony at many gay weddings, the couple recesses out to a contemporary/pop song.

**The Yichud.** *Yichud* is the Hebrew word for "seclusion." The *yichud* is a ritual at a Jewish wedding, in which the newly married couple spends a period of time secluded in a room by themselves immediately following the ceremony. This practice has become very popular with same-sex couples that take a few minutes to be alone with each other immediately following their marriage! During the *yichud,* the guests sign the Foundation Covenant as witnesses to the marriage. The Covenant is often later framed as art (and conveniently can serve as a guest book.)

*Guests are standing for this wedding*

# Informal Weddings

I've planned many weddings at which the fifty-plus guests stood for ten- to twenty-minute wedding ceremonies. There was select seating for elderly family and friends but generally no more than twenty or so chairs up front. These types of weddings have a nice casual vibe to them, and often the marriage ceremony seems to unfold very organically.

Informal ceremonies can work well—and they can fail. If you are considering this option, here are some tips:

- Truly keep the ceremony no more than fifteen minutes long.
- Even though this is casual, make a plan about the partners' processional. Options including coming in from two different directions and meeting in the middle, walking down a central aisle, and walking down the sides of each aisle and meeting in the middle.
- Make sure you have a coordinator designated to clear the aisle or form an aisle when it's time for the processional.

- Greet your guests with a drink (which could be champagne, sparkling water, or lemonade) when they arrive, and plan to allow the guests to mingle for about fifteen minutes before your true ceremony start time.
- Don't mingle with your guests during that time, or your ceremony will definitely start late!
- Place the ceremony musicians where they will be easily visible by your coordinator so the coordinator can cue the processional music when the time is right (it's sometimes hard to see the musicians when most people are standing!).
- Make sure you have "an escape route" and destination after the recessional if there's no receiving line. Otherwise you and your partner will get mobbed by your guests and a receiving line will happen spontaneously.

If you follow those guidelines, an informal ceremony can work out very well and can set the tone for a casually fun and upbeat reception. Gay couples seem to enjoy this style of event because it breaks with tradition and because many of them don't want the grand-entrance processional of conventional wedding ceremonies.

Two of my grooms held their wedding ceremony in their gorgeous living room with thirty friends and family members (who had been drinking champagne and having nibbles for forty-five minutes). The twenty-five-minute ceremony was scripted and delivered by a celebrant who, after asking them to complete individual questionnaires and spending quality time learning about their lives together, beautifully told the story of their relationship. One of the readings was from the book *Giovanni's Room,* one of the groom's favorite novels.

# Formal Religious Ceremonies

*A ceremony in a Congregational Church*

Those members of the clergy authorized to perform same-sex marriages include: some rabbis (who often require you to be a member of his or her temple), United Church of Christ ministers, Metropolitan Community Church ministers, Unitarian ministers, non-denominational ministers, interfaith ministers, and a few others.

## Faiths Allowing Same-Sex Marriages

**United Church of Christ:** The United Church of Christ was the first mainstream Christian church to fully support same-sex marriage. UCC has over five thousand churches and more than one million members.

**Jewish:** Reform Judaism embraces same-sex marriage and rabbis can perform ceremonies

**Metropolitan Community Church:** Churches in the Metropolitan Community Church fully embrace and welcome lesbian, gay, bisexual, and transgender people and allow for gay marriage.

**Unitarian:** Unitarian ministers perform same-sex marriages and have many "open and affirming" congregations.

**Quaker:** The willingness to perform gay marriages varies by meetinghouse, but there is some acceptance and performance of same-sex marriages among Quakers.

## Faiths Allowing Limited Same-Sex Marriage

**Episcopal:** In the Episcopal Church, priests are authorized to bless same-sex wedding ceremonies but not declare the marriage official or sign the marriage license. Episcopal priests in Eastern Massachusetts can fully marry same-sex couples without conditions.

## Faiths Disallowing Same-Sex Marriages

**Methodist:** The United Methodist Church will not conduct same-sex marriages and will not allow them to be held in their churches.

**Lutheran:** Lutheran ministers will not conduct same-sex marriages and will not allow them to be held in their churches, but are authorized to bless the unions.

**Baptists:** Southern Baptist and Conservative Baptist churches will not conduct same-sex marriages, nor will they allow them to be held in their churches. Some American Baptist churches are open and inclusive.

**Catholic:** The Catholic Church will not conduct same-sex marriage ceremonies or allow them to be held in their churches. The Catholic Church continues to fight the legal recognition of homosexual couples.

**Presbyterian:** The Presbyterian Church does not sanction same-sex marriage, and a Presbyterian minister cannot perform a same-sex union ceremony like the marriage ceremony.

## Ceremony Processional Options

There are many ways you can set up your wedding-ceremony space (especially at a gay wedding, because there are no expectations of you!). The space can truly set the tone for your wedding.

## Option 1: Traditional—The Central Aisle

The conventional ceremony setup is what you are used to if you grew up going to a Catholic or (most) Christian churches. The chairs are arranged on either side of a central aisle. Most church weddings, even gay weddings, use a central aisle.

In a gay wedding, the couple (rather than just the bride) usually walks down the central aisle to the front of the room where they are married in front of their guests. We've planned some (but not many) weddings at which the clients use the central-aisle approach. In this case, sometimes the brides or the grooms will be escorted by family members, but it can be a challenge to decide who will be the last partner to process. More often, the wedding party walks down the aisle followed by both grooms or both brides (alone and holding hands), so as to avoid the traditional role of the bride being the primary focal point.

## Option 2: Central Aisle With V-Shaped Seating

*A V-Shaped Seating Arrangement*

This arrangement is essentially the same as option 1, but the V (or chevron)-style chair setup allows for more people to see the couple and creates a feeling of intimacy. I've had some couples choose this option just to do something a little different and to offer guests a tiny tweak to the traditional without being too wild and crazy.

# Option 3: Central Aisle With a Semi-Circle

*A semi-circle seating arrangement.*

The semi-circle setup takes Option 2 one step further, allowing for greater visibility of the couple and creating a stronger feeling of intimacy.

This arrangement works well with outdoor ceremonies or spaces where there's plenty of room to make wide semi-circles. We've seen this approach be particularly successful on a beautifully landscaped lawn, or adjacent to a tented area. The semi-circle creates a feeling of community and of sharing the space together.

# Option 4: The Spiral

*A Spiral Arrangement*

In this ceremony setup, chairs are arranged in a spiral, winding inward toward the center where the couple will marry. The nice thing about the spiral is that the couple can pass every individual guest during their processional and recessional. And the ceremony can be seen by all since it's held in the middle of the spiral.

As planners, we only experienced this setup once and it was effective. The brides were seen by all of their guests, but the problem is that some of the guests are staring at butts or looking at backs during the ceremony. This approach also makes it difficult to capture great photographs.

## Option 5: Ceremony-in-the-Round

*Chairs set up for a ceremony-in-the-round*

A ceremony-in-the-round is similar to the spiral arrangement, but in this situation all the chairs are set a few rows-deep in a circle. There are small breaks in the circle for aisles and the couple uses those to approach the ceremony space during the processional and recessional. The advantage again is that everyone can see the marriage from all directions.

One of my clients processed in together into their circle, holding hands to the Beatles song, "All You Need is Love." They walked around the circle acknowledging their guests. In each of four corners of the circle, there was an altar with candles and symbols representing the four elements. The couple was married in the middle but had blessings at each altar. This traditional pagan wedding and handfasting ritual was beautiful. You can easily adapt this setup for whatever kind of ceremony you are having.

# Option 6: No Central Aisle

*A seating arrangement with no central aisle*

Best for smaller weddings, in the "no aisle" arrangement all the chairs are set up in long (typically curved) solid rows with no open space in the middle. Each partner walks down one side of the seating and crosses over to meet in the middle with the other. The advantage to this is the symbolism of "meeting in the middle" and coming together.

I like this setup in weddings of fifty or fewer guests. The guests feel close to one another since an aisle does not separate them, and the brides or grooms can each have a separate entrance from which to come together.

A disadvantage is that you have to can only exit down one side!

## Option 7: Multiple Aisles

A multiple-aisle setup, like others, is designed to use the "meet-in-the-middle" metaphor. It's a nice option if the couple does not want to walk in together, yet one does not want to be the last to go and make the "grand entrance" à la the Bridal March. In this setup, the couple can walk down separately yet simultaneously.

*This multiple-aisle approach that Jen and I used.*

*Each bride walked down one side of the pool.*

As with the "no aisle" arrangement, a disadvantage of having multiple aisles is that you'll have to choose only one aisle down which to exit.

This is the setup we chose for our wedding and I'm so glad we did. We chose it because I didn't want either of us to process down last, even with our families. I wanted us to process at the same time. It was just what was important to me. In our case, each member of our bridal party walked down the aisle one at a time. The doors closed for us, and then we walked down our respective aisles simultaneously, and met in the middle.

## Framing the Ceremony Space

Unless you are getting married in front of a beautiful fireplace, staircase, or a stunning natural backdrop, it's a good idea to "frame" the ceremony space and create a sense that it's sacred.

The photos that follow depict different ways to frame the ceremony. I find that creating a special space for the wedding ceremony adds a specialness to the event and works nicely for photographs.

*Wedding arch*

*Buckets of tall floral arrangements*

*Pedestals*

*A chuppah (in Jewish tradition)*

## Sacred Documents

I love Ketubahs, Foundation Covenants, and other sacred wedding documents. I think they are elegant and can reflect the personality of the couple. For example, at Sarah and Jane's wedding, the language on the Ketubah was in Hebrew (because Sarah's Jewish), in Korean (because Jane's Korean American) and in English. And it was absolutely gorgeous!

Traditionally, the Ketubah is signed by the couple, their rabbi/ officiant and a few witnesses before the wedding. The Foundation Covenant and Quaker Marriage Certificate are signed by the couple and their officiant during the ceremony, and by their guests witnessing the covenant, after the ceremony. As I mentioned earlier, a Foundation Covenant can also substitute as a guest book.

We had a Foundation Covenant at our wedding, and it was produced by Daniel at Modern Ketubah. His work is absolutely stunning, truly best seen in person. Ours completely exceeded our expectations. Unlike a guest book, which typically is left with many empty pages, the Foundation Covenant will grace the walls of our home, reminding us of the love and support of our friends and family. Wrote one of my cousins, "You are pioneers and adored by all. Thanks for the wonderful day and the sunshine. Love you."

That's a nice reminder. Thanks, Barb!

Be sure to work with a talented and brilliant officiant who can talk to you about your options for sacred wedding documents.

*Foundation Covenant*

*Ketubah*

## Vows

A question I'm often asked by couples is, "should we write our own vows?"

Jen and I talked about it and decided not to write ours on our own. We figured that there were plenty of gorgeous vows out there—why reinvent the wheel when we might not be so eloquent?! But I must admit, I love it when I'm standing in the back of the room watching the couple reveal their deeply personal, handwritten vows to each other for the first time. There's almost nothing more sweet.

I planned a gay wedding officiated by a dear friend of the grooms'. She came into Boston from California quite prepared for her role. But try as I might, I couldn't get the grooms to focus on their role - writing their own vows (they had a lot going on in their lives!). Even at the wedding rehearsal, they still had nothing scripted—nothing like the last minute! The next day, the ceremony was flawless: the grooms processed into a live "Trumpet Voluntary," holding their son's hand. Their friend delivered a stunning ceremony script and the grooms presented before the other the most personal and heartfelt vows I'd ever heard. There was not a dry eye in the room, and it was so clear why these two gentlemen were absolutely perfect for one another.

If you choose not to write your own vows, your minister, celebrant or justice of the peace will have a nice selection of choices for you. And there are loads of books on the subject (I have one my clients frequently borrow). But here are some of my favorites, starting with our own vow:

Today I love you completely, as I did yesterday and will tomorrow.
I will be there for you always.
I will share in your dreams, delight in your joys, and comfort you in your sorrows.
I will be your confidant, your counsel, and your friend.

When you are not within my sight, you will be within my thoughts.
You are my life, you are my joy;
You are my love, and today, you are my wife.


I, _____ take you _____ to be my partner/husband/
wife/spouse for life.
I promise above all else to live in truth with you,
And to communicate fully and fearlessly.
I give you my hand and my heart
As a sanctuary of warmth and peace
And pledge my love, devotion, faith, and honor,
As I join my life to yours.


I, _____, take you _____
My friend, my love, and my lifelong companion.
To share my life with yours,
To build our dreams together,
To support you through times of trouble,
And to rejoice with you in times of happiness.
I promise to treat you with respect, love, and loyalty
Through all the trials and triumphs of our lives together.
This commitment is made in love, kept in faith,
Lived in hope, and eternally made new.

I promise to encourage your compassion,
Because that is what makes you unique and wonderful.
I promise to nurture your dreams,
Because through them your soul shines.
I promise to help shoulder our challenges,
For there is nothing we cannot face if we stand together.
I promise to be your partner in all things,

Not possessing you, but working with you as a part of the whole.
Lastly, I promise to you perfect love and perfect trust,
For one lifetime with you could never be enough.
This is my sacred vow to you, my equal in all things.

## Tips for Writing Your Own Vows

If you do decide to write your own vows, it can be really lovely, but do it right. Follow these tips and you'll have your guests and your partner in tears!

- Decide whether you will be keeping the vows secret from your fiancée or collaborating on joint vows.
- Write the vows in your own voice. The tone of the vows should sound like you and something you would say, not stiffly written.
- The vows should ideally have some personal meaning and might include a personal promise, such as that of a client who wrote "I promise to walk with you at sunset every chance I get."
- The vows should include a promise and say something nice about or to your partner.
- The vows may include a story or anecdote but if so, should be kept short and sweet.

One of my pairs of brides had a ceremony co-officiated by an interfaith minister and a district court judge/noted civil rights attorney. Their deeply personal, handwritten vows included phrases like, "I promise to take you to Italy at least once a year." They processed out to a live flute and guitar version of "You Are the Sunshine of My Life" by Stevie Wonder. Goosebumps!

## Ceremony Readings

I know that some people, myself and Jen included, have difficulty reconciling their sexuality with the religious traditions that they grew up with. We know that there are many religious institutions that don't perform or recognize gay marriages.

The good news, though, is that there are some passages from the Bible and other sacred texts that may bring you comfort and that you may find appropriate for your wedding. Here are some examples from the Bible:

### Ruth 1:16–17 (Appropriate for Lesbians)

But Ruth said, "Entreat me not to leave you or to return from following you; for where you go I will go, and where you lodge I will lodge; your people shall be my people, and your God my God; where you die I will die, and there will I be buried. May the Lord do so to me and more also if even death parts me from you."

### 1 Samuel 18:1–4 (Appropriate for Gay Men)

When David had finished speaking to Saul, the soul of Jonathan was bound to the soul of David, and Jonathan loved him as his own soul. Saul took him that day and would not let him return to his father's house. Then Jonathan made a covenant with David, because he loved him as his own soul. Jonathan stripped himself of the robe that he was wearing, and gave it to David, and his armor, and even his sword and his bow and his belt.

### 1 Corinthians 13:1–8a (Appropriate for Gay Men and Lesbians)

If I speak in the tongues of mortals and of angels, but do not have love, I am a noisy gong or a clanging cymbal. And if I have prophetic powers, and understand all mysteries and all knowledge, and if I have all faith, so as to remove mountains, but do not have love, I am nothing. If I give away all my possessions, and if I hand over my body so that I may boast, but do not have love, I gain nothing. Love is patient; love is kind; love is not envious or boastful or arrogant or rude. It does not insist on its own way; it is not irritable or resentful; it does not rejoice in wrongdoing, but rejoices in the truth. It bears all things, believes all things, hopes all things, endures all things. Love never ends.

Many Jewish couples, straight or gay, use the Seven Blessings. Here is a contemporary version of the Seven Blessings:

## The Jewish Seven Blessings, Contemporary

May your marriage enrich your lives.

May you work together to build a relationship of substance and quality.

May the honesty of your communication build a foundation of understanding, connection, and trust.

May you respect each other's individual personality and philosophy, and give each other room to grow and fulfill each other's dreams.

May your sense of humor and playful spirit continue to enliven your relationship.

May you understand that neither of you is perfect; may your love strengthen when you fall short of each other's expectations.

May you be best friends, better together than either of you apart.

Here are a few other popular, secular readings:

## The Apache Wedding Prayer

Now you will feel no rain,
for each of you will be shelter for the other.

Now you will feel no cold,
for each will be warmth for the other

Now you will feel no loneliness,
for each of you will be companion to the other.

Now you are two persons,
but there are three lives before you:
his life, her life, and your life together.

May beauty surround you both
on the journey ahead and through all the years.

May happiness be your companion
to the place where the river meets the sun.

Go now to your dwelling
to enter into the days of your life together.

And may your days be good
And long upon the earth.

## "A Sacred Space" From the Tao Ta Ching by Lao Tzu

Your love requires space in which to grow.
This space must be safe enough
To allow your hearts to be revealed.
It must offer refreshment for your spirits
And renewal for your minds.
It must be a space made sacred
By the quality of your honesty,
Attention, love and compassion.
It may be anywhere,
Inside or out,
But it must exist.

## Other Great Readings

Some other popular readings you might want to consider include:

- "For Good" from the soundtrack to the musical *Wicked*
- "This Marriage—Ode 2667" by Rumi
- "Touched by an Angel" by Maya Angelou
- Excerpts from *Leaves of Grass by* Walt Whitman

Interestingly, the most popular reading at gay-wedding ceremonies is not from a celebrated poet or inspirational novel, nor from a sacred text or a religious tradition. The most popular gay-wedding ceremony reading has tremendous meaning. It's historical. It's beautifully written. It speaks volumes about the significance of a marriage. And it was written by a lawyer ...

Well, a judge actually. The most popular reading during gay wedding ceremonies is part of the ruling that legalized gay marriage in Massachusetts (the first state to legalize gay marriage). It was written by Judge Margaret Marshall from the State Supreme Judicial Court. While this is by no means the whole ruling, the passage below is the long version and is often excerpted into smaller readings:

> Marriage is a vital social institution. The exclusive commitment of two individuals to each other nurtures love and mutual support; it brings stability to our society. For those who choose to marry, and for their children, marriage provides an abundance of legal, financial, and social benefits. In return it imposes weighty legal, financial, and social obligations ... Without question, civil marriage enhances the "welfare of the community." It is a "social institution of the highest importance."

Marriage also bestows enormous private and social advantages on those who choose to marry. Civil marriage is at once a deeply personal commitment to another human being and a highly public celebration of the ideals of mutuality, companionship, intimacy, fidelity, and family ... Because it fulfills yearnings for security, safe haven, and connection that express our common humanity, civil marriage is an esteemed institution, and the decision whether and whom to marry is among life's momentous acts of self-definition.

I hope you consider including a piece of history in your wedding ceremony.

## What's in a Name?

I was recently corresponding with a couple that sent me a note on their ceremony draft. One of the grooms wrote, "Jeff and I have been together for more than fourteen years. After a life of saying 'my partner' I'd love, at long last, to say, 'my spouse.'"

And so he did. Language is a funny thing. I know another unmarried gay couple together more than ten years that refer to themselves not as partners, but as lovers. That term is not for everyone but it works for them.

What words to use in referring to one another is a big decision for gay and lesbian couples. I get asked all the time about how the officiant will declare them at the conclusion of the ceremony. I now declare you ...

- legally married,
- lawfully married,
- partners for life,
- married partners,
- husbands/wives to one another,

- spouses for life,
- something else?

Jen and I chose "legally married." That phrase felt right for me, because in my mind the legal element of the wedding is so important. We live in a state where our marriage is legal and I want that word to be heard loud and clear. But that's not always the case, and not everyone wants the declaration to sound even remotely "political."

Once you're actually hitched, how will you refer to your spouse? Many couples I know initially cringed at using the words "husband" or "wife." Dan Savage, author of the "Savage Love" advice column, still refers to his partner Terry as his "boyfriend," even though they were married in Canada a few years ago. I had a hard time adjusting to the word "fiancée," and that took quite a while to feel natural. Many couples still use the term "partner" because it's what's comfortable and familiar. And to be perfectly honest, I occasionally catch myself referring to Jen as "my girlfriend!" Whoops!

Since I've been married, I've been using the word "wife" as often as possible, just to get used to it. Instead of saying, "Hey Jen," sometimes I'll say "Hey wife"—and she does the same. It's certainly an adjustment but a worthwhile one.

And finally, what about the last name? Many people keep their names, but I've had several clients and a friend invent entirely new names, some of which were not remotely similar to either of the old names. That's kind of fun—as you begin a new life together, you do so with a new name. And of course you can hyphenate your names. Sometimes this works out nicely (if the names flow together), but sometimes it's awkward.

So what did the gay-wedding planner do? We merged our names. Jen wanted to use a hyphen and I did not, so Jen is now Jennifer Coveney-Smith and I am Bernadette Coveney Smith. We simply couldn't come to an agreement on the hyphen, so we agreed to disagree and are living happily with that decision.

# Chapter 12:
# Showtime: Photos, Music, Makeup!

The next part of wedding planning is to book vendors who, in most cases, work only one wedding per day, and in many cases, one wedding per weekend. These are the vendors who book-up first, and you will have a better selection if you reserve these vendors well in advance (I suggest booking them at least six months before your date). Photographers, DJs/bands, videographers and hair and makeup stylists are on this list.

As you start to get proposals from vendors you meet with, you'll also start to see lots of vendor contracts. Some of these contracts are simple while others are very long. Here are some elements that are standard in vendor contracts:

- Date, time, and location
- Contact names
- Vendor requirements, which may include table, power supply, a meal, parking, etc.
- Payment terms
- A Force Majeure (Act of God) clause, releasing them from liability in the event of a natural disaster or other catastrophic situation

- A release of images provision, allowing your wedding planner or photographer to use images from your event for promotional purposes
- A limitation of liability clause, in the rare instance of damage

## Photographers

Wedding photography is an investment. Don't skimp on it! Your photos are one of the few things that will remain long after your wedding is over. You probably already know that most wedding photographers shoot with digital cameras rather than film, but if you have a preference you'll want to address it with the photographers you interview. Here are some other questions to ask yourselves before you begin to call photographers:

Are you planning to see each other before the wedding? I asked you think about this issue earlier, and it bears repeating here. Most gay couples I've worked with have had their formal group photos taken before the ceremony so that they can immediately enjoy cocktail hour with their guests. (As a point of reference, many straight couples first see each other when the bride walks down the aisle and have their formal photos taken during cocktail hour.)

Do you want a photographer who will shoot all day? You might like to have the photographer take shots of you and your partner getting ready for the wedding, and, as mentioned above, take formal photos before the ceremony. On the other hand, perhaps you'd be happy with coverage of just the ceremony and reception.

What photographic style are you drawn to? Do you prefer photos that look like fine art or that capture little moments? Do you like photos that look like they could be from a fashion magazine? Think about the kind you like best.

Are you planning to walk down two aisles or enter your wedding ceremony from two different directions? If so, you may want to consider asking the photographer to bring an assistant.

Will you need lots of formal group shots that include your wedding party and family members?

Will you want a wedding album? Wedding albums are provided by most photographers (as an additional service), but you can also create your own beautiful, archival-quality album through a Web site like www.AlbumBoutique.com

Once you've answered the above questions, you'll be much better prepared to meet a photographer. Keep in mind you will be spending six plus hours with the photographer on your wedding day and should like his or her personality.

Above all, you should click with the photographer. If you feel like you'll have a good relationship with someone, there are some requisite questions to ask in addition to reviewing his or her portfolio. Here's a standard list of questions to ask when interviewing a photographer:

- Have you shot a gay wedding before?
- How would you describe your style?
- How many photos do you shoot at a typical wedding?
- Do we get proofs of the images?
- Are proofs digital proofs or paper proofs?
- What level of editing do you provide photos before we receive them? Do you do color correction, crop out EXIT signs, and the like?
- Do we get full use of high-resolution images after the wedding?
- Do we book an album through you or can we make our own?
- How long does it take for you to give us the high-resolution wedding photos?
- How long does it take for you to produce an album?
- What is your backup plan in case of emergency?
- Do you offer an assistant and if so, for what price?

- Do you offer an engagement photo shoot and if so, for what price?
- How many weddings do you shoot in a weekend?
- How is your pricing structured?

## Videographers/Wedding Films

There are lots of ways to save money on your wedding. But do not skimp on a photographer and videographer.

Jen and I made both photography and videography priorities for our wedding. Wedding videography has long held the stereotype of being tacky, with a giant spotlight taking up too much room on the dance floor and annoying guests. We've all seen the handheld, shaky, horribly edited footage with cheesy glamour-shot type designs. There's a good reason that videographers have a bad reputation.

These days, however, there are some video artists who can truly capture your wedding memories forever. The best videographers in the industry are trying to escape the stereotype and prefer to be called "filmmakers." Like your photographs, a good wedding video is an investment, something you will treasure for years to come and share with your loved ones. I know that our child will one day love our wedding film.

Let's start with some basic definitions:

## Film

You can touch and feel film. You can hold it up to the light and see images. Film has been around for decades and can create amazing images. It's also expensive, complicated and an extra hassle to edit. It's rarely used in wedding film production.

## Video

Video can come on a reel of tape or it can be digital. It records your images and does not require processing or development. It is easy, fairly uncomplicated and the standard in the wedding industry.

# Super 8

In short, Super 8 is a type of 8mm film (not video). Shooting with 8mm film produces a stylishly grainy look. A wedding video can be shot solely on Super 8, but a more versatile option is to combine the Super 8 with digital HD or SD footage to create a wedding video that really captures your day.

## HD (High Definition) and SD (Standard Definition)

HD is the enhanced video (not film) standard. It is superior in color and resolution (sharpness and detail) to SD.

Some notes about HD video:

- The equipment is more expensive than that for SD video, and not as many companies offer it.
- It is very hard to shoot true HD video in low light. HD cameras struggle in low light and it may require artificial lighting to capture HD.
- Because of the lighting and the enhanced definition, makeup appears different on HD video from how it looks in person. Airbrushed makeup will look more finished and perfect on HD video and traditional makeup may look overdone.
- HD video must be screened on an HD TV with an HD player or the resolution cannot be seen.

## Videographer Interview

When interviewing videographers, get the following information:

- Is the videographer's business gay owned?
- Has the videographer you worked with gay couples before or shot any gay weddings?
- What's is the videographer's style?

- Ask to see an entire wedding video (not just a trailer). The trailer is just the highlights: be sure to see how the videographer covers an entire wedding.
- While watching the video, pay attention to the sound quality, especially during key moments. You'll want to remember the vows and toasts. Is the bestie's toast loud and clear? Can you hear the sweeties say "I do"?
- Ask the videographer whether his or her equipment is wireless. Does he or she have wireless mics? Does he or she have wireless lights?
- Speaking of lights, will a giant spotlight on the dance floor kill the mood? Or worse yet, a giant spotlight in your guests' eyes?
- How will the videographer capture the wedding music? Can he or she plug into a DJ or band mixing board?
- What kind of equipment does the videographer use?
- Does he or she shoot in high definition or standard definition?
- How many shooters do the videographer bring to each wedding?
- How long is the turnaround time for an average wedding video edit?
- How long are the final edited videos?
- How many DVDs do you receive as finished products?
- How do you order extra copies and for what cost?
- On site at the wedding, how does he or she relate to the wedding photographer? Are they generally in each other's way or not?
- Does the videographer generally contact the photographer for still wedding photos to use in the wedding video?
- What is the business' emergency plan in the event of equipment failure or illness?

# A DJ or a Band?

Music is obviously a critical element to your wedding. You're going to have to figure out whether you prefer a DJ or a band, and which you can afford. Lots of couples have a bias against DJs, expecting that they'll bring props like boas and inflatable guitars, have their logo or signage on everything, and play line-dances like the Macarena and the Chicken Dance. Ninety-five percent of my clients explicitly say, "I don't want to hear the Chicken Dance at my wedding."

Who can blame them?

A band can really get the guests up and moving on the dance floor and its energy is infectious, but they have to eat dinner, too, and sometimes the whole crew will disappear without putting on a CD for dinner music. And all you hear is the scraping of forks on plates. Not cool.

Let's go through some pros and cons of a DJ versus a band:

- The DJ can obtain and play virtually any song you want to hear at your wedding. The band will have a limited repertoire and will usually only be willing learn one or two songs for your wedding.
- Many DJs have a reputation for being cheesy. Many will bring props, such as inflatable instruments, cowboy hats, and boas. The have been known to hang tacky promotional signage, talk too much, and seek to be the center of attention. Bands seldom exhibit such inappropriate wedding behavior.
- The DJ will cost somewhere between five hundred and fifteen hundred dollars (on average), whereas bands typically start at thirty-five hundred dollars and go up from there.
- The DJ is only one person to feed and can easily provide music during a dinner break. The band is a group of five plus people that you'll have to feed.

Bands have been known to take long dinner breaks without providing backup music.

- The energy created by a DJ will be limited to the music he or she plays. A band physically creates energy that is infectious and can get your guests up and dancing.
- Both DJs and bands can provide music for the ceremony and cocktail hour. In most cases, you will be charged extra for this service. Typically, only a few band members will perform during the ceremony and cocktail hour, with the rest arriving for the reception.

If the ceremony is in the same room as the reception, the DJ or band may have to do some, if not all, of their setup prior to the ceremony, leaving their sound equipment in a corner of your ceremony space. This might be necessary in order to insure that music is available from the start of the cocktail hour. This may not bother you, but keep in mind that that the gear can be an eyesore.

## Music Issues

Regardless of who provides the music for your wedding, there are some things you'll want clear before you start interviewing DJs and bands.

What are the approximate times for structured activities? These would include guest arrival-time, ceremony start-time and event end.

How formal is this wedding? Is this summer semi-formal or black tie? In short, how do you want your DJ or band members to dress?

Do you expect a lot of announcements? Announcements may include introductions, first dance, other formal dances, toasts, garter and bouquet toss, and cake cutting. Specific announcements are not necessary to determine ahead of time unless there will be formal introductions. If so, you'll to think about (later, not now) who will be introduced, and how?

Will there be any planned activities during the event? Will you need your musician(s) to accommodate a structured dance performances (such as by a drag queen or fire dancer), a song sung by a loved one, or some other special activity?

Do you want the DJ/Band to take music requests from guests during the event?

Will you be providing the DJ or band with a "do *not* playlist?"

Will you be providing the DJ or band with a "*must* playlist?"

When I was twenty-four-years-old, I was invited to a gay commitment ceremony. My friends who lived in Atlanta decided to marry on the beach in South Carolina. They used all local vendors in the area and it was a beautiful event. Unfortunately, the reception was marred by a local DJ the hired. The DJ made derogatory comments about the brides and their guests and had to be physically removed from the reception. Can you imagine? That event is one of the reasons I started my company. I tell that story as a reminder of the importance of coming out immediately with all of your vendors and of clarifying the vendor's attitude toward you and your wedding.

Now that you've determined some of your requirement for your music provider, you're better prepared to interview DJs and bands. Be sure to ask these questions:

- Have you performed at any gay weddings?
- How many songs are in your repertoire or library?
- What kind of equipment do you use?
- How long have you been performing?
- How would you describe your style?
- What kind of backup equipment do you have in case of emergency?

- What is the contingency plan in case of emergency illness or injury on or near the wedding date?
- Do you provide music for the ceremony and cocktail hour? Is there an extra fee for this?
- Do you provide sound equipment for the wedding ceremony? Is there an extra fee for this?
- Do you have a secondary sound system to be used in the cocktail hour space?
- Are you willing to learn to play or buy songs that I want to hear at my wedding? If so, how many?
- Do you typically take requests from guests? How do you handle requests?
- How do you manage the flow if guests aren't dancing?
- Do you provide music when you take a break? What kind of music?
- Do you bring any props or signs?
- Do you provide any lighting or AV services?
- How much time do you typically need for setup? Can you set up within an hour, during the cocktail hour, if needed?
- Do you have a set playlist that you use for most weddings?
- How do you dress for a wedding?

## The Role of the Emcee

Whether you choose a DJ or a band, be sure that you're comfortable with the emcee. This individual is going to be managing the flow of your wedding. A good emcee is critical! Make sure the emcee is someone who will be unobtrusive and not talk too much, but who will be personable, professional, and clearly heard.

## The iPOD Reception

An increasing number of couples are making playlists on their iPOD and using that as their wedding soundtrack. Using an iPOD can be successful and it can fail miserably. If done properly, this can be a major savings for a couple, though it may not be worth the hassle of setting it up right. Here are my tips:

- Ensure that the venue has a sound system you can plug the iPOD into. If there's no sound system, be prepared to rent one.
- Does the sound system carry into the space used for the cocktail hour? If not, is there a secondary sound system?
- Who will be your emcee? Be sure to assign someone the job of making announcements throughout the evening so the flow is well directed.
- If you are having more than fifty guests, be prepared to rent a microphone and amplifier for the ceremony officiant, readers, and emcee. You will definitely need one.
- As you put together your playlist, change the setting that creates a gap between songs. Make sure there's no gap between songs, not even a brief gap. Believe me when I tell you that even a five-second gap can kill the momentum on the dance floor.
- Create multiple playlists for the sake of the person who will be in charge of pressing "play." I was once handed an iPOD right before the wedding with three playlists that said "wedding." I wasn't sure which playlist to use and had to bother the brides to ask. Make one playlist called "cocktail hour" another called "first dance" (with just one song in the playlist), another called "cake cutting" (with just one song in the playlist) and so forth, so that the keeper of the iPOD will be crystal clear on how to use it effectively.

## Hair and Makeup

Many of our brides (and bridegrooms!) have said to us, "I feel like I should wear makeup but I don't want to be all dolled up or look like a clown."

All of this is perfectly okay, of course. Another concern they've expressed is that if they hire a traditional hair and makeup stylist that they won't look or feel like themselves on their wedding day.

The best solution is to try out several vendors and see who listens to you most closely. This is called a trial. Who is going to make you look like the best version of yourself?

Before looking for assistance with wedding hair and makeup, I advise couples to look at images for examples of hair and makeup that they like and think would be a good fit for their hair and features. They should bring those photos to their meeting with the hair and makeup stylist(s).

My first suggestion is always to ask your personal hairstylist whether he or she travels onsite for wedding hair. If you already have a relationship with that person, it's great to be able to have that familiarity and peace of mind on your wedding day. Keep in mind that just because she or he is your personal stylist doesn't mean you should skip a trial.

Before you get in touch with potential stylists, have the following issues worked out in your own mind:

Are you paying for hair and makeup for any members of your wedding party? This is a personal decision and is not required. Some couples pay for hair and makeup for their wedding party as a gift to them.

How many people need hair and makeup? The total number of people may include the two people getting married, family members, and wedding party members. Regardless of whether you are paying for their hair and makeup services, you should ask your wedding party members if they would like access to this service.

Do you want the stylist(s) to stay throughout the wedding to provide you with touch-ups? There is a premium for this service, of course.

Do you want hair and makeup to be done onsite where you are getting ready, or are you willing to travel to your stylist? I *strongly* advise against traveling for this service on your wedding day. Allow yourself to be pampered and let the vendors come to you!

During your trial, bring a camera and ask the following questions:

- What is the stylist's experience with hair and/or makeup for gay weddings?
- Does the stylist provide both hair and makeup, or one or the other?
- How many people can he or she provide hair and makeup to without bringing an assistant?
- What time does the stylist arrive onsite on the wedding day?
- What's the order for hair and makeup for the wedding party?
- What brand of products does the stylist use?
- Does he or she ever stay throughout the event for touch-ups?
- How can I make sure that my hair/makeup will last throughout the event?
- How long does the stylist typically spend on makeup per person?
- Does the stylist provide airbrushing? (if applicable).

After the trial, make sure you get photos taken of yourself sporting the finished product so you can compare it with your appearance after other trials, or so you can look back and get excited about your wedding day!

And make an extra note: you'll spend a lot of time with your stylist—how is his or her personality?

**Transgender Tip:** If you are a transgender bride, be sure to come out when calling hairstylists and makeup artists. Not only are you looking for someone who is comfortable with you, but you may also require someone who has experience styling hairpieces or applying makeup to transwomen.

# Chapter 13:
# Dreaming in Logistics: Catering, Cake, Flowers, Transportation

The next group of vendors you hire are those who can generally provide services for more than one event per day. For example, it's not unusual for florists to have multiple weddings on an evening or over a weekend. They have the staff to make it happen. These vendors can be hired four to six months before the wedding

## Catering

*Passed hors d'oeuvres*

Our loved ones are still talking about how good the food was at our wedding. No boring, overcooked chicken for us. Our guests had lobster and filet mignon, and the food didn't cost an arm and a leg. Your guests are going to spend at least a good two hours eating at your wedding (including the cocktail hour) so you might as well give them something memorable.

Before calling caterers, answer the questions below yourselves:

How many guests do you expect at your wedding? You can provide a range, but by now you should have a good idea of how many to expect.

Are the ceremony and reception in the same location? This is an important issue for timing. If the ceremony is onsite, the caterer may have to set up earlier than normal so as to be well out of the way before guests begin to arrive. Depending on the venue, the caterer may also pre-set dinner tables and pull them to the side of the room to be screened off for the ceremony.

Are you serving champagne or anything before the ceremony? Traditionally, gay couples greet their guests before the ceremony with butler-passed sparkling wine or water. This lets the guests know that this is not your ordinary kind of wedding and helps take the edge off before the festivities begin.

What is your favorite kind of food? Are you a foodie or do you like classic American comfort food? Do you have a favorite restaurant that is a special place for you both? Do you have a favorite ethnic food that's crucial to include on your wedding menu? We've had clients ask the caterer to base their wedding-dinner menu on that of one of their favorite restaurant.

Do you want to have a long cocktail reception, a buffet, food stations, a family-style meal, or a plated dinner? Let's explore this a bit. There are pros and cons to each, but the decision is often based upon the type of energy you want to create at your wedding.

**Cocktail Reception** This is a big party with most guests standing and limited seating. To do thiseffectively, you should have a shorter event (otherwise guests might get bored or tired). You'll also want to make sure that you keep the food flowing all night so your guests feel as though they've eaten a proper meal. The most effective way to do this is to create a lounge area for your guests with tables and chairs (either provided by the venue, or rented by you). This type of wedding is casual and informal, but the cost of a cocktail reception-style event is not necessarily much less expensive than a more structured party. You still have to provide a lot of food and staff.

**Buffets and Food Stations** These are nice because they're casual, they get your guests out of their seats and provide an opportunity for mixing, mingling and getting to know one another. You'll also offer a greater variety of foods at a buffet or food station than you probably would at a plated dinner. Food stations can be themed or interactive. An example of this is a pasta station in which pasta is sautéed to order depending on the sauce or veggies chosen. In this scenario, guests are told, table-by-table, to go up to the buffet or stations while those at other tables wait. With buffets, you also run the risk of running out of a certain dish, while with plated dinners, the number of portions are controlled in the kitchen before service. Typically, two to three tables at a time can go up. As a point of etiquette, the head table (or newlywed table) goes first, followed by immediate family.

The downside to buffets and food stations is that not everyone eats at the same time and some of your guests (for example, those at the last table to go up) may be waiting forty-five minutes for food. Guests eat more at a buffet or food station, so food may run out (I've had this happen to me as a guest when my table was the last called to the buffet). A common misconception is that a buffet or food station will be less expensive than a plated meal. If it is, it's only slightly less expensive. Caterers have to provide more food for buffets or food stations, but they also provide fewer staff. In the end, the prices of the two are fairly comparable.

**Family Style** In this case, servers place large platters of food at each table and those platters are passed around among the guests, family style (just like it sounds). This type of service can be really nice in the sense that it creates intimacy. Although it sounds like a fun idea, in execution it doesn't work that well at weddings. There's not much table space for all of those platters, and the food cost ends up being high because so much food is provided.

**Plated Dinners** These are served tableside by waitstaff that bring the food to you. Guests stay seated and there's little interaction with other tables. This is a more formal option. In general, there will be one first course (appetizer, soup, or salad) and one second course (an entrée), followed by a cake course, although there may even more courses depending on your style and budget. If the first course is a salad or something that's not temperature sensitive, you can have that pre-set at each place setting so it's there when guests sit down for dinner. This will save service time. Generally, your guests will not get a choice of food for the first course and the cake course, but instead will be served something that you've pre-selected and believe to be universally appealing. A good caterer who is well staffed will set most of the meals within just a few minutes of one another. Plated dinners are, in my opinion, the most elegant way to feed your guests at a wedding reception, though you may find them slightly more expensive than the other options.

*Artfully presented plated dinner*

Do you want the caterer to provide the dessert or wedding cake? Many caterers have in-house pastry chefs who can prepare for you a variety of desserts, possibly even including a wedding cake. My favorite caterer here in Boston has made the most magnificent wedding cakes for my client. I'll never forget the one with mascarpone cream … mmmm.

Do you want the caterer to provide the bar? A full-service caterer should be able to provide you with a bartender, ice, and liquor liability insurance, and should also be able to order the alcohol and mixers. In short, a full-service caterer can do it all. Some caterers just take care of food, however, and you'll have to hire a bartending service and work with a liquor store for the rest.

Do you want to coordinate linen rentals through the caterer? The caterer will have to order some rental items for your wedding. Depending on where the wedding is, the rentals may include tables and chairs, glassware and flatware and even ovens. Since they are ordering a number of things already, it's easy enough for them to add linens to the order. A good caterer should have swatches of linens in his or her office so you can choose some you like. The nice thing about having the caterer coordinating linen rentals is that he or she will know exactly how many tables there are to drape, thereby saving you time and energy. The disadvantage is that the caterer often marks up this service, slightly more than if you had made arrangements yourself directly with the rental company.

Do you have many vegetarians or guests with special dietary restrictions? You may not know this off the top of your head, but if you do happen to know that you have vegans and/or those with nut or shellfish allergies among your guests, this is something to bring up when you actually speak with a caterer.

Do you want to ask guests to pre-select their entrees? Prior to the wedding, the caterer will want to know how many of your guests will want a particular entrée. You can ask your guests to note how many of each option they would like on their invitation-response card. Then you tell the caterer the number of each chosen entrée, and once you've set up table assignments, the number of each entrée at each dinner table. However, it's increasingly common *not* to ask your guests to choose their entrées in advance, but rather to present a small set menu at each place setting. On the menu, guests will see the pre-selected dishes for the first course and dessert course, and a short list of entrées to choose from as a second course. Here's an example:

First course:
Mixed Green Salad with Granny Smith Apples, Dried
Cranberries and Chevre

Second course:
Grilled Statler Breast with a Mushroom and Chestnut Sauce
Or
Lemon Glazed Grilled Scallops Served over Smoked Tomato
and Fennel Puree
Both Served with
Roasted Root Vegetables
Mashed Cauliflower Drizzled with Lemon-Chive Butter

Dessert:
Wedding Cake and Crème Brûlée

You should know that this set menu option is more expensive (an extra five to ten dollars per person) since the caterer has to be prepared with more food and you will have to create and print a menu (some caterers provide these menus).

Alternately, without any pre-selection or tableside ordering required, each guest can be given a plate with a dual entrée—that is, one of each, à la surf and turf. Some guests may just want the surf *or* the turf, however, and the caterer should be prepared to accommodate this request.

Once you've given serious thought to your own food and service desires, you can start researching caterers. These are the questions you should ask when first talking to caterers (this list assumes that the wedding is in a place where you supply your own caterer):

- Is this a gay-owned business?
- Have you worked on any gay weddings before?
- Have you worked in xxxx venue before?
- Are you a full-service caterer? Can you provide buffets, plated dinners, and food stations?
- Do you coordinate rentals, including linen rentals?
- Do you offer set menus or require all of your entrées to be pre-selected in advance? Can the wedding entrée be a duo of two proteins?
- Can you provide bartenders, liquor liability, ice, beer, wine, liquor, mixers, and other bar supplies?
- Do you make wedding cake or other desserts?
- Can you accommodate special dietary needs such as gluten-free, vegan, vegetarian, and/or nut-free meals?

At this meeting, you should be prepared with answers to the questions I provided and the caterer should offer to put together a proposal for you. Once you've received a few proposals and made any changes to better suit your needs or budget, you can schedule a tasting.

## Staying in Season

One of the many things that is wonderful about the locally grown, sustainable agriculture movement is that wedding food tastes so much better. I am thrilled that my clients are demanding locally grown food at their events.

One of the tricks about serving food from local sources is that the wedding menu may not be set until right before the wedding day—in order to serve what is local and available that week. I worked with two wonderful guys from Manhattan who chose one of Boston's top restaurants for their wedding. But because the menu was seasonally changing and they weren't able to make a final trip, they sent me in the Tuesday prior to choose among their possible entrées. Yum!

The great thing about seasonal dishes is that they put everyone in a good mood. For example, strawberries are everywhere in the summer, and who doesn't love a ripe and juicy strawberry? Nothing says summer quite like it. And I think there's something sexy and mildly suspenseful by seeing a wedding menu that simply says "seasonal vegetables."

Any great chef—be it at a restaurant, caterer, or function facility—will know exactly where to source his produce and how to create a sexy, seasonable menu for you and your guests.

## The All-Important Tasting

It's so important to taste the food you will eat on your wedding day. You should note that some caterers won't do a tasting unless you've already signed a contract with them. Some will charge a fee, around fifty or one hundred dollars, that is credited toward your bill if you book with them. And some caterers or venues will schedule monthly or quarterly group tastings with their clients. Keep in mind that in some cases, you'll be choosing a caterer before you actually get to taste the food. This is certainly not ideal, but you'll have to rely on your intuition, reviews, and how enthusiastic you are about the initial menu.

Whenever I'm working with clients, the tasting is one of my favorite parts of the planning process. Of course! Free food, yes, but the look in a couple's eyes when they actually sit down and taste the food they may be having on their wedding day is pretty special. Especially, of course, if it tastes good and they are comfortable and happy with the process. The tasting makes the wedding begin to feel ultra-real.

Your tasting should include at least a few of the passed hors d'oeuvres that are part of your most recent wedding proposal, as well as two or three of your first course, entrée and side selections. If the caterer or venue is providing wedding cake, you should be able to taste that, too (though I admittedly prefer to go on cake tastings separately). An effective tasting should answer many of the questions about your wedding day and the flow of the event. Here are the things you should note on your tasting:

- How is the food presented?
- Are hot dishes served hot and cold dishes served cold?
- Is the plate presentation appetizing?
- Are the hors d'oeuvres easy for your guests to eat? Side note: I personally hate skewers— they are awkward and unattractive!
- Do the flavors pop? Are they complex? Is the food absolutely divine?
- Do the courses flow well together? Is there too much of one kind of protein or do you have items that are very divisive (like goat cheese, which I love)? I'm not saying you need to change or eliminate those items!
- Is there a nice balance of selections for vegetarians and carnivores?
- Will there be any in-season changes to the menu?
- When is the latest date you can make a change to the menu?

- If the caterer will be managing your rental order, ask whether the linens have been picked out. Make him or her show you swatches!
- Are the plates you're eating off the same plates you'll be using on your wedding day? Are the flatware and glassware the same?
- Will you be having decorative charger plates? Chargers are larger plates placed at each place setting onto which your napkin, menu, and some or all food courses are placed. *Side note: Say yes! Chargers are lovely!*
- What is their standard napkin-fold? Do you like it?
- Be sure to get assurance that every last person on the service staff will treat you, as a same-sex couple, right!
- If you are choosing a set menu (rather than pre-selected entrées), does the caterer or venue provide menu cards? What is the heading at the top of the cards?
- Think about when you will be having a champagne toast. Do you want the champagne pre-set at the dinner table?
- What is the approximate timing for dinner? How long does it take the caterer to get through three courses if serving a plated meal?
- Is there a separate cake-cutting fee?
- Can the caterer provide tableside wine service? Do you want him or her to?
- Confirm whether the fee includes a staff gratuity. Side note: a gratuity for the staff is typically not included when you are working with an outside caterer.
- Confirm the bar setup if you are hosting the bar: does the caterer charge a flat fee per person or by consumption? (Maybe you're lucky enough to bring in your own alcohol.)

- If possible, taste your wedding wine with the food. If the venue provides the food and bar, then ask the staff for a wine tasting. If you're bringing in your own caterer and bar, then bring your own wine to the tasting!
- What time will the caterer begin setup?
- If you haven't already done so, arrange with the caterer a location for your gift table, guest book, and escort cards.
- Confirm the flow of the space if the ceremony is held onsite: where does everyone go for cocktail hour while the room is being arranged for dinner? To what degree will the dinner tables be set up prior to the ceremony and how will they be hidden discreetly?
- If you don't have a wedding planner to manage the caterer, who will be your day-of-event go-to person? What authority does that person have to act as an event planner and liaison with the other vendors like the DJ and photographer?

If you are having a plated dinner and asking guests to pre-select entrées, you'll need a system for keeping track of which meals will need to be brought to which tables. Once those invitation-response cards start coming in, you can begin using the following chart set up in a spreadsheet:

| TABLE NAME: | | | | | |
| --- | --- | --- | --- | --- | --- |
| Name | Entrée A | Entrée B | Veg | Child | Notes |
| | | | | | |
| | | | | | |
| | | | | | |
| | | | | | |
| | | | | | |

|  |  |  |  |  |  |
|---|---|---|---|---|---|
|  |  |  |  |  |  |
|  |  |  |  |  |  |
|  |  |  |  |  |  |
|  |  |  |  |  |  |
| **Totals:** | 0 | 0 | 0 | 0 |  |
| **Total at Table** | 0 |  |  |  |  |

## Vendor Meals

You have to feed the people who are working at your wedding: not the bartender and waitstaff, but the musicians, the wedding planner, photographer, videographer and anyone else who will be working your wedding for more than five hours. Most such vendors require a meal in their contracts.

The good news is that in most cases, you won't have to pay full price for a vendor meal. Most caterers and venues will sell you a vendor meal for a reduced price, typically between thirty and forty dollars. Vendors know which caterers and venues provide the best vendor meals, but it's good for you to ask your caterer what the vendor will be eating. I've been served everything from cold boxed-lunch sandwiches to the entrée portion of the guest's dinner (and everything in between).

## Booze

There are so many debates over serving alcohol at a wedding. Whether to have a bar, and what to provide if you do, is full of controversial issues!

Let's start with some definitions:

**Host/Open Bar:** A host/open bar means that the hosts of the wedding pay for the bar and the guests do not. Host bars are typically charged on consumption (what guests drink) or at a flat rate per guest. A host bar can be either a full bar (described below), or a limited, signature bar.

**Cash Bar:** At a cash bar, guests pay for their own alcoholic drinks.

**Full Bar:** A full bar means that guests may choose from a full choice of beers, wines, and alcoholic drinks. This can be a host/ open bar or a cash bar.

**Limited Bar:** Guests may choose from a limited choice of alcoholic drinks, which typically include a red or a white wine, several beers, and one signature cocktail.

Here are some helpful hints on managing the bar situation— and your bar budget!

1) Create a signature drink. Your signature drink might be a drink that relates to your color theme, the season, your favorite spirit, or something else entirely, but it's nice to have a fun signature cocktail that reflects your personality. Even if you don't offer a full bar, offering a signature cocktail is classy and a great conversation starter. Plus, having a signature drink but no other liquors can lower your overall alcohol budget, because many guests will switch to typically lower-priced beers and wines.

2) It's a nice idea to offer a signature "mock-tail" for your non-drinking guests (who may enjoy something more interesting than a club soda with lime).

3) Although toasts are traditionally with champagne or sparkling wine, you can certainly do a "toast-in-hand" instead. Many people don't even like champagne!

4) Ask the venue representative if there is a policy against serving shots of hard liquor. Many venues do, and it's a good idea to check, especially if you are expecting some wild guests or rowdy cousins who may cause trouble at your gay wedding!

5) Tip jars are confusing and fairly tacky so don't have one at the bar at your wedding!

6) There is enormous debate about whether a cash bar is in poor taste. I've noticed that some families and cultures are very accepting of them, and some families always have cash bars at their events. Others do not, and it's just what they and their guests are used to. Every wedding I ever went to as a guest had an open bar, but I've had some clients opt for a cash bar and the

guests didn't bat an eyelash because that is what they had come to expect.

7) If you'd prefer not to have a cash bar but an open bar is out of your budget, then a) cut your guest list and/or b) opt for a limited bar.

**A Note on Signature Cocktails:**

Signature cocktails, as I mentioned above, are a way to personalize your wedding. They can compliment the color scheme or your wedding theme, if you have one. They can have fun names that represent you and your personality. You can rename a popular drink with something more representative of the two of you. For example, you could have a signature cocktail called the "Ptown Partini" if you were having your wedding in Provincetown or having a beach-themed wedding.

I also encourage my clients to have a little party during the planning stages with a few close friends (pick those with great palates!). Then mix up a few cocktails that are contenders for your signature cocktail and see what the group thinks. During our wedding planning, we had such a party which I called, simply enough, our Signature Cocktail Tasting Party.

We weren't sure what theme to work with: the Irish theme of our wedding, or our color scheme (one of our colors was navy). We ended up making and serving a bunch of horrible-tasting drinks, including some with blue curaçao and coconut rum! Never again! But it was a great excuse for a mini party ...

In the end, the winning cocktail was something called the Wild Irish Rose. It wasn't navy blue but it did go with our Irish theme. Our recipe is amended from the original and we tried several iterations before settling on the following:

In a cocktail shaker, combine the following over ice:
2 oz Jameson's Irish whiskey
1/2 oz grenadine
3/4 oz fresh lemon juice

Shake and serve straight up in a chilled martini glass with a sugared rim. It's delicious and pretty in pink (though that was the only pink to see at our wedding).

To take it even further, I am admittedly sometimes a bit ridiculous and over-obsessed with details, so as our cocktail hour began and these drinks were passed to our guests, an Irish band performed the classic tune "My Wild Irish Rose." Even if no one but Jen and I made the connection, it still meant something to us!

So, go make a signature cocktail! Do something fun! Experiment! It's these kind of personal touches (especially the ones that allow you to catch a little buzz) that make wedding planning fun.

*Signature cocktails being passed*

## Choosing the Perfect Wedding Wine

When planning a wedding, there are so many indulgent details to obsess over. Jen and I had so much fun indulging in private, at-home wine tastings with potential wedding wines. It was great couple-bonding and a big obsession of mine (though certainly a fun obsession)! Our wedding venue provided its own catering and wine list. We took a look at the list, tried a few, were vaguely disappointed and decided to choose our own and have it ordered. We tried to stay within the ten to fifteen dollar per bottle price point, because the venue will mark up a special order by as much as 300 percent. This was a fun process ...

Choosing the right wine for your wedding can be a wonderful theme-related detail. For example, I had clients last year that had a travel-themed wedding. Their custom-designed wedding invitations were boarding passes and their table names were personal photos of places the couple been together on vacation. The details were great, up to and including their red wine selection, Boarding Pass Shiraz, selected not only because it was thematic but also because they enjoyed the wine.

During the course of wedding planning, it's not unusual for my clients and I to share some wine. I worked with two gentlemen last fall that always had a beautiful bottle of Chardonnay in their home (never red wine, for fear a spill would damage the beautiful Jonathan Adler furniture). Together we shared many bottles of wine, and picked out wines for their wedding and holiday party. Through them, I discovered the delicious Liberty School Chardonnay— and its gorgeous, buttery color and flavor—robust and fruity, yet with a nice, crisp finish.

When it came time to choose our own wedding wines, I went right for the Liberty School, not even noticing that the name complimented our theme (we were getting married on the 3rd of July, after all). Their Cabernet is equally as good as their Chardonnay and Jen's mom, a red-wine aficionado, loves it. I am a big fan of New-World styles of wines and big, bold reds. Their Cabernet is softer than some; it tastes full of berries with a kick of pepper. I think it's actually a very fun, summery Cab.

I recently went food and wine tasting with clients from Manhattan. Together we tasted an exquisite, affordable white called McManis Viognier. The first thing you notice is the wine's peach aroma. This is an outstanding wine value at about twelve dollars per bottle, and my clients chose it for their white offering. The next day, Jen and I had a bottle and decided to switch to the McManis for our wedding, especially since it would go great with the lobster on our menu. I highly recommend this wine.

When planning your wedding, don't forget to choose wine you love . It's an inexpensive detail that can speak volumes about you and it's a great way to celebrate on your anniversary!

## Your Wedding Cake

I'm hungry already. I am a firm believer that wedding cake should be delicious and need not be dry, cold, or sugary. The best cake-makers book up well in advance, so don't procrastinate about this delicious process! Small cake shops generally limit themselves to making ten or fewer wedding cakes per weekend, while larger shops can handle many more.

To get you started in selecting a wedding cake, there are a few "terms of art" you should know:

**Buttercream:** Buttercream is a smooth, creamy frosting made out of butter. It tastes great, is easy to serve and can be piped to decorate the cake.

**Fondant:** Fondant is a type of icing generally made out of sugar, corn syrup, and gelatin. It's rolled with a rolling pin into a thin sheet that gets draped over the cake. It has a smooth, nonsticky finish, can be painted, colored, and decorated with virtually anything. Most people don't like the taste of fondant, but because buttercream is generally under it, I ask my caterers to remove the fondant prior to cutting and serving it to guests so the cake tastes its best with just the buttercream. Fondant is easily removed. Note that fondant makes the cake more expensive.

**Ganache:** Ganache is a sweet, rich chocolate, denser than mousse but less dense than fudge, which can be used as icing or filling.

**Piping:** Piping is a way of decorating a cake using a pastry bag and various metal tips. With piping, you can create beading, flowers, weaves, and lots of other designs on the cake.

**Filling:** The filling is the yummy goodness between each layer. Filling flavors include lemon, raspberry (or other fruits), coconut, chocolate mousse, and lots more.

## Taste the Cake!

Naturally, one of my favorite parts of wedding planning is cake tasting, and I've had plenty of wedding cake in my six years of planning gay weddings. It never gets boring to me. Be sure you go on several cake tastings before you make your final decision. The taste can vary widely. Some buttercreams are gritty and overly sugary. Some cakes themselves are dry. Fondant almost universally tastes bad—but looks great! Taste the cake! It's fun.

# The Cost of Cake

Wedding cakes are almost universally priced by the slice, typically three dollars and up per slice.

Serving cupcakes can be slightly more cost effective, depending largely on their size. They are typically two dollars and up per unit.

# Fresh versus Frozen

Believe it or not, some cake-makers still bake a cake, freeze it, ice it, freeze it again, and then thaw it out before the wedding. The problem with this technique is that sometimes the cake isn't quite defrosted and tastes cold and dry. Bakers who do this often produce dozens of cakes per weekend.

The best bakeries make their cakes fresh, do a lower volume of business and thus charge more for their cakes. It's a personal decision you'll need to make but be sure to ask the bakery when they make the cakes.

# Layers

I encourage my clients to have each layer be a different flavor, but with the same flavor buttercream on the outside. Maybe one layer is a chocolate cake with raspberry filling and another layer is carrot cake. The different flavors won't cost you anything extra and they give your guests some variety.

The tradition of saving the top layer of cake in the freezer and eating it on your first anniversary seems to be evolving over time. I love that some of the bakeries I take my clients to offer a complimentary mini anniversary cake on the couple's first anniversary. It's great for customer service and keeps you from having to eat stale, dry cake. Plus, that means you get to serve and eat the top layer on your wedding day.

## Prettying the Cake

I really like using fresh flowers to decorate an otherwise simple cake. If you do this, be sure to identify whether the florist or baker is in charge of this detail. If it's the florist, confirm that the delivery person puts the flowers on the cake, or assign someone else to do it. If it's the cake designer, he or she will take care of the fresh flowers when the cake arrives. One way or another, make sure you have a plan for this.

## Questions for the Bakery

When you start contacting bakers, be sure to ask the following questions:

- Is this a gay-owned business?
- Do you have experience with gay weddings?
- How many flavors of cake and filling can we taste at the tasting?
- What's the delivery fee?

While at the tasting, follow up the these queries:

- Can I see a portfolio?

- Do you make custom-designed cakes?
- Do you have "stock" designs?
- How many days prior to the wedding do you make the cake?
- How long prior to the wedding start-time do you deliver the cake?
- How many cakes do you produce a weekend?
- What ingredients do you use?
- How many servings are there per tier of cake?
- Do you offer fresh flowers as a garnish?
- Do you provide an anniversary cake?
- Do you offer desserts in addition to cake?
- Do you sell cake toppers?

## Instead of Wedding Cake

Recently I've had an increasing number of clients, gay and straight, who opt for a wedding dessert other than wedding cake. Now, this is not to say that wedding cakes have gone the way of the dinosaur—far from it—but about one-third of my clients are mixing it up a bit.

Cupcakes (the obvious substitute) are a good choice.

Strawberry shortcake is a colorful and delicious option.

Some couples like to provide a group of miscellaneous cakes from their favorite bakeries.

If you are of the mind that a cake cutting is a fun wedding tradition, do you instead cut the pie or strawberry shortcake? If you wish to, of course!

## Coffee and Cake Stations

Some couples have the cake served at a coffee and cake station rather than brought to each table (tableside). I like this idea because it gets your guests UP and OUT of their seats and can encourage more mingling and interaction and get them on the dance floor. Another advantage of a cake station is that not everyone eats cake and you can order up to 10% less than your actual guest count because there will be those who don't eat the cake.

## Flowers

The quickest and simplest way to decorate a space is through flowers. I love flowers. Jen is good at keeping our house full of flowers, candles, and music. I noticed this early on in our relationship, and it had such an impact on me that I made sure to mention it in our wedding ceremony. Anyway, I love flowers.

A container (the florists don't say "vase") of fresh flowers instantly warms up a room, bringing oxygen and light. Weddings of course can be over-the-top with flowers, but there are some ways to keep it simple. Here are some important points when first considering your wedding flowers:

- What are your wedding colors and themes? The florist will want to know this so he or she can suggest flowers accordingly.

- What is your budget for flowers? In general, I suggest to couples that for a wedding with fifty guests, you can count on spending between twelve hundred and fifteen hundred dollars on flowers. For one hundred guests, expect to spend around two thousand to twenty-five hundred dollars, and up. This budget largely depends on the space you are using and how much it needs to be decorated.
- What's your style? Some floral designers have a specific style. Some really shine at fluffy, ruffley, monochromatic designs (a very classic look), while others do their best work with textured, gardeny designs (a very rustic, garden-chic look). Still others are at their best with contemporary designs featuring exotic flowers. It's a great idea to clip images of floral designs you like. Figure out what look you're going for and make sure you find the designer who excels with that look.
- Who will need personal flowers? Personal flowers include bouquets, nosegays (mini bouquets), corsages, and boutonnieres.
- Will you designate your ceremony area with flowers? If you think about a traditional wedding ceremony, the ceremony itself is often held under a chuppah or in front of an altar space. If you choose to do something else, it's always a nice idea to somehow designate the space as a sacred ceremony space, and it's usually the florist who provides the flowers and ceremonial elements. If your ceremony is in front of a fireplace, mantel, nice bookcase, or even a beautiful staircase, you can get away without a lot of floral additions.
- Choose flowers that will be in season on your wedding day and will last a day or two once cut. Your florist will be able to tell you what will be fresh on your wedding date. I love hydrangea, for example, but it withers within a few hours of being out of water. Hydrangea is

one thirsty flower, and thus might not be a great choice for a wedding bouquet if it's out of water all day.

- While purchasing seasonal flowers is the most cost effective approach, note that most flowers can be purchased most times of the year. Flowers are grown all over the world, in South America, the Middle East, and of course, Holland. If the flower you are desperate to have for your wedding isn't in season where you live, chances are your florist can still get it if you are willing to incur the extra cost.

- Remember that floral design can be hard work. It's more than just cutting flowers and putting them in a container. Flowers need to be picked, shipped, cut, have their leaves removed, and in some cases, be de-thorned. They have to be treated for a few days to open up to their fullest. They have to be kept in a cool place. My point is that there is hard work behind what you pay for your wedding flowers. You're paying for both the flower cost and also for the florist's design and overhead.

Here is a quick checklist of all of the different kinds of flowers used for wedding. These are the details you'll discuss during the initial consult with the floral designer:

- Number of bouquets for the bride or groom
- Number of boutonnieres for the bride or groom
- Number of attendants needing bouquets
- Number of attendants needing boutonnieres
- Mothers (include stepmothers)
- Fathers (include stepfathers)
- Grandmothers
- Grandfathers
- Ushers
- Hostesses
- Children (flower girl/ring bearer)

- Honorary attendants (reader, soloist, etc.)
- Officiant
- End-of-aisle decorations
- Ceremonial items (chuppah, arch, gazebo, pillars, etc.)
- Table centerpieces
- Food tables (buffet, cake, etc.)
- Other tables (escort-cards table, gift table, etc.)
- Other room décor (entryways, staircases, mantles, doorways, pillars, etc.)

## Selecting a Florist

Once you've come up with a floral budget and an idea of your needs, it's time to call around for proposals. You should ideally contact two or three vendors and ask the following questions:

- Is this a gay-owned business?
- Have you worked with gay couples before?
- Do you require a minimum floral budget?
- Have you worked in xxxx venue before ?

*Two rustic bouquets*

*A delicate boutoneirre*

Once you've gotten a short list of potential florists, you can set up a time for an in-person consultation. For these meetings, prepare yourself with answers to the questions we discussed above and ask the floral designer the following questions:

- Where do you source your flowers?
- Do you provide candles, linens, or other decorative items?
- Do you rent floral containers or do we keep them?
- Do you rent any ceremonial elements, such as arches, chuppah, or pedestals?
- How many weddings do you work in a weekend?
- Do you sell aisle runners?
- Do you sell petals?
- What is the delivery and set-up charge?

*Example of a low centerpiece*

*Example of a high centerpiece*

## Transportation

I've noticed that gay wedding transportation rarely involves limos, stretch Hummers, or Rolls Royces. Why? Traditionally, those vehicles are used to transport the wedding party to the ceremony and then the reception. But when there's no wedding party and the ceremony and reception are in the same location, no limos are needed! It's a great way to save money.

Of course that's not always the case. I have rented limos to transport the wedding party on a number of occasions. Even our wedding required a small fifteen-passenger shuttle bus. In my experience, drivers for transportation companies are among the most homophobic vendors. When you are calling to book transportation for your gay wedding, it's very important that you specifically ask for a driver who will be gay-friendly. I've had good experiences with the sales representative, but when it came to the actual driver, I've heard some really homophobic comments.

You may also find yourself in a situation where you have to provide guest transportation. This can be a big expense. Big charter buses can easily cost six hundred dollars, but they have no greater capacity than some more whimsical vehicles. For example, when my clients need to provide guest transportation, instead of renting charter buses, I rent trolleys. These are easy to rent here in Boston and in other bigger cities. Your city or area may have something equally fun. How about a double-decker bus? A school bus? They're both great ways to give your guests a taste of the area. Something out of the ordinary provides just a touch of whimsy that your guests will love.

*A trolley will delight your guests*

## Tips for Tipping All Your Vendors

Before tipping anyone, check carefully to see what is included in the bill ... limo companies, caterers, and venues providing valet and coat check services may already have a line item for gratuity!

**Caterers:** Look for a gratuity line item for both the service staff and the bartender. If it's not included, leave thirty-five to fifty dollars per server and for the catering manager, and 15 to 20 percent of the bar bill for the bartender(s).

**Limo:** Leave 15 to 20 percent of the bill.

**Musicians:** Tip each musician twenty five dollars or more.

**DJ:** A DJ should receive 15 percent of his fee, if they do not own their own company.

**Hair & Makeup:** Tip the stylists 15 to 20 percent of their fees.

**Valet:** Tip the valets fifty cents to one dollar per car.

**Coat Check:** Coat checkers should receive fifty cents to one dollar per coat

For exceptional service, you may, but need not tip your:

- Photographer/Videographer
- Floral Designer
- Planner
- Cake-maker

# Chapter 14:
# Fun With Paper: Your Wedding Invitations

Having booked a venue and officiant and settled upon all of your major vendors, it's time to focus on invitations. By now you've decided whom to invite. Even if you go with whimsical save–the-date cards, keep in mind that invitations truly set the tone for your wedding. If possible, you should carry through your wedding colors and/or theme on the invitations. The save-the-dates and invitation can be part of the process of teasing your guests about what they may expect on your wedding day.

What I like about the invitation is that it can be part of a cohesive theme that is carried throughout your wedding stationery: on the ceremony program, escort cards, table name signs, menus and so on. How cool to see a seamless design throughout. It's just classy and elegant. And I'm a big fan of green weddings, so even if you skip the ceremony program and the menu, you can still have a cohesive design theme.

Before you go invitation shopping, ask yourself these questions:

1. What is your budget for invitations? You can find invitations online for less than two dollars per set,

but the price can (literally!) go up to thirty dollars or more per set. Many couples spend between five and ten dollars per set.

2.  What is your color and/or theme? Start with one or both of these items and weave those design elements into your invitations, your ceremony program, your dinner menu, your escort and/or place cards, your table name signs, your thank-you notes and so forth.

3.  What is the vibe of your wedding? If your invitation is traditional and elegant, your guests will assume it's a traditional and elegant wedding. Conversely, if your invitation is more fun and casual, your guests will get that vibe as well.

4.  Do you want to go shopping for invitations at a store so you can touch and feel them? Or would you rather sit behind your computer and purchase invitations online? The bonus of ordering online is that there's an enormous amount of variety and you don't necessarily have to come out each time. You can also get samples sent to you from most major online invitation makers.

5.  Do you care about an eco-friendly invitation? Getting green invitations can be as simple as using paper that's FSC- (Forest Stewardship Council) certified or having them printed on recycled stock. Your invitations can actually have embedded seeds that can be planted by your guests. That's pretty cool if it's your thing!

6.  Do you want invitations that have "gay" imagery? By this I mean, do you want invitations that show silhouettes of two brides and two grooms, or feature any kind of rainbow symbolism? If you do, then you should consider looking for them at a Web site such as GayWeddings.com or OutVite.com.

7.  Do you prefer a certain printing method? These are the primary options:

o **Engraving:** Grooves are cut into a printing plate that's used for printing images on paper called engravings. These invitations have a raised appearance and you can feel the grooves on the back of the paper. The process creates a very formal, and traditional invitation. Engraving is expensive.

o **Thermography:** Thermography is also a raised printing method, but it is less expensive than engraving. The thermograph printed invitation has a puffy paint-type finish because that's essentially what it is: the finish is shiny and glossy and does not press through the paper.

o **Flat printing:** Either digital or offset, this is the most common print method where the lettering and images are flat—there is no physical texture to the invitation. Flat printing can produce outstanding results with more contemporary designs or any sharp, clean designs.

o **Letterpress:** Letterpress is a very popular and luxurious printing method. With letterpress, the raised surface of the type is inked and then pressed against a smooth substance to obtain an image in reverse. The type is literally pressed into the paper and you can feel the indentations. Letterpress is a manual process, and it requires that each sheet be fed one at a time. Because most letterpress equipment can only print one color at a time, it's best suited for one- and two-color invitations. If the invitation has a large image, the paper may need to go through the letterpress twice to avoid spottiness. Letterpress is a beautiful but expensive option.

With joyful hearts

we ask you to be present

at the ceremony uniting

*Christopher Alan*

and

*Matthew Jan Lewis*

on Monday, the thirteenth of September

Two thousand and ten

at six o'clock in the evening

Independence Hall

1801 West 40th Street

Burlington, Vermont

Reception will immediately follow

## Stationers

A stationer is someone who sells stationery. You've probably heard of the stores Papyrus and the Paper Source, which are examples of national stationers that sell wedding invitations. When you visit a stationer you'll be able to see and touch many different kinds of wedding invitation options. It's a good thing to do just so you have a sense of what's out there. In addition to inquiring about the type of printing a stationer provides, here are some other things to ask when meeting with a stationer:

- How long is the turnaround time for an invitation suite?
- What types and/or font options can I choose from?
- What ink color options can I choose from?
- How many different colors can an invitation suite contain?
- Is any of your paper made from recycled materials?
- Do you provide proofs? If so, are they digital proofs or paper proofs?
- Do you provide assembly and mailing service?
- Do you provide a calligraphy service?

## What's in the Envelope?

- **The invitation itself:** The invitation is the largest element and it includes the names of the couple, the location of the wedding and the date and time. It may also include the names of parents if they are hosting and requested attire. It should not include RSVP, registry information or a wedding Web site URL. This information appears on the logistics card.
- **Logistics card:** The logistics card may include information about other wedding weekend activities, the URL of your wedding Web site, directions, and so forth. I tell my clients who are not inviting children

to their wedding to include "Adults-Only Reception" or similar language on their logistics card and an offer to coordinate child care.

- **RSVP card or postcard:** The RSVP card or postcard should be provided with a stamp or stamped envelope. This reply card is for guests to indicate whether they will attend, and in some cases, to indicate their entrée choice. Sometimes, the card will ask guests to mark whether they will participate in other wedding-weekend activities. A tip for response cards is to write a tiny number on the back of each (preferably with a blacklight pen) that corresponds with a guest name on your wedding spreadsheet. This is helpful should your guests forget to fill in the space for their name on the card, or if their handwriting is illegible.
- **Directions:** Directions may be on the logistics card or, if very detailed, they may require a separate enclosure, which may be a color map.
- **Tissue Paper:** Tissue paper is often used to separate the invitation from the rest of the invitation suite.

## Assembling, Addressing, and Mailing

You can get away with mailing labels on your save-the-date cards, but it's best to handwrite or hire a calligrapher to address your invitations. Other tips:

- Don't buy stamps until after the invitation is assembled—you may be surprised by how much the invitation weighs or to learn that its shape affects the weight.
- If you are sending any invitations overseas, don't forget to buy airmail stamps for those invitations. Be aware that you may not be able to stamp the response card.

- There are lots of online resources (I like WedAlert. com) for how to address invitations for traditional couples, but not many for same-sex couples, and it's confusing to figure out how to address invitations to LGBT couples. Here's the rundown on how envelopes are addressed:

**Outer envelope:** If they are an unmarried couple, the names should be on two separate lines, in alphabetical order. For example:

Ms. Jennifer Coveney
Ms. Bernadette Smith
14 Willow Street
Boston, MA
02110

**Inner envelope:** Ms. Coveney and Ms. Smith

**Outer envelope:** If they are married with different last names, the names should be on the same line in alphabetical order. For example:

Ms. Jennifer Coveney and Ms. Bernadette Smith
14 Willow Street
Boston, MA
02110

**Inner envelope:** Ms. Coveney and Ms. Smith

**Outer envelope:** If they are married with the same last name, the names should be on the same line, in alphabetical order. For example:

Mrs. and Mrs. Bernadette and Jennifer Coveney-Smith
14 Willow Street
Boston, MA
02110

**Inner envelope:** Mrs. and Mrs. Coveney-Smith

By the way, the above information is just an example, that's not our real address!

## Invitation Verses

My favorite online resource for invitation verses is VerseIt. com. You'll be able to choose from a variety of verses depending upon your special circumstances. Your invitation may (or may not) set forth the involvement of parents, whether there are children involved, whether it's a destination wedding and so forth. Here's what Jen and I used on our wedding invitation:

> Jennifer Marie Coveney
> and
> Bernadette Mary Smith
> joyfully invite you to share
> in their celebration of marriage
> on Friday, the third of July
> two thousand and nine
> at six-thirty in the evening
> The Exchange Conference Center
> 212 Northern Avenue
> Boston, Massachusetts
> Reception will immediately follow

Note that we chose the words "joyfully" and "celebration" because we wanted to immediately communicate that this was to be a big, fun party.

# Example invitation with couple and parents inviting guests:

Together with their parents

Christopher Alan Zucker

and

Matthew Ian Lewis

request the honour of your presence

at their marriage

on Monday, the thirteenth of September

Two thousand and ten

at six o'clock in the evening

Independence Hall

1801 West 40th Street

Burlington, Vermont

Reception will immediately follow

# Example invitation with couple inviting guests:

Christopher Alan Zucker

and

Matthew Ian Lewis

invite you to share in the joy

when they exchange marriage vows

and begin their new life together

on Monday, the thirteenth of September

Two thousand and ten

at six o'clock in the evening

Independence Hall

1801 West 40th Street

Burlington, Vermont

Reception will immediately follow

## Invitation Etiquette

There are a lot of details to keep in mind as you mail out your invitations. Some of the most common questions I get are:

- When should I mail the invitations? You should mail your invitations about six to eight weeks before the wedding (definitely eight weeks if you have a B-list or are sending invitations overseas).
- When should I request a response? Request a response within two to four weeks after the send date.
- Who gets an invitation? Each unmarried adult guest should receive his or her own invitation even if they are roommates, siblings, or BFFs.
- Do the names of children appear on the envelope? If you are inviting children, the names of the children should be on the outer envelope.
- What goes on an invitation? As I mentioned earlier, your invitation itself is simply an invitation and should *not* include any of the items described above in the logistics card.
- Do I need two envelopes, an outer and an inner? Traditionally, the invitation is in an envelope within an envelope. The reason for this was to keep the inner envelope clean when invitations were hand-delivered on horseback. Now you can get away with just one envelope (and save a tree).
- Do invitations need to be hand-addressed? Handwritten invitations are the tradition and they are what many of the more conventional members of your guest list will expect. I am giving you permission to use nicely typed mailing labels (preferably clear) if you must.

# Web Resources

If it's easier for you to shop online than in a store, my favorite sites for wedding invitations are:

- GayWeddings.com
- OutVite.com
- ScissorPaperStone.com
- OsloPress.com
- PapeterieStore.com
- WeddingPaperDivas.com

You may need to ignore heterosexist language that you might find on some of these sites, but even if you do encounter it, I promise you that all of these sites are gay-friendly.

# Chapter 15:
# Weddings on a Dime

The economy is hitting everyone hard. A tight budget doesn't mean that your wedding design needs to be seriously compromised— you can still plan a stunning wedding. One trend we've noticed since the economy has gone south is that couples are still planning spectacular weddings, but they are inviting fewer people. Since food and beverages are typically the mostly costly elements of a wedding, a smaller party can mean significant savings.

Some more cost-saving tips …

- Plan a winter wedding or a wedding on a Friday night or a Sunday brunch—you may get vendor discounts (you should definitely ask!), and food and beverage minimums may be lower. Avoid high demand dates such as Valentine's Day and New Year's Eve. Consider having an afternoon event, at which alcoholic beverage consumption will be significantly lower than at an evening event.
- If you are wearing one, choose a wedding dress from a selection of bridesmaid dresses, not from the typical wedding gown department.

- Skip some of the stationery elements that are costly and environmentally wasteful. This means: no favors (which are often left behind), no ceremony programs, and perhaps a seating chart instead of escort cards. You can even skip save-the-date cards.
- If you have guests who love to drink, consider an open bar with only wine and beer, plus perhaps one delicious signature cocktail.
- Consider putting a time limit on the hosted portion of the beverage service. Close the bar thirty to forty-five minutes before the end of the event and serve only soft drinks and coffee.
- If you are hosting a full bar, consider limiting the grade of liquor. Hosting a mid-grade liquor selection rather than a combination of mid- and premium-grade liquors can trim 10 to 15 percent off your bar bill.
- Have your ceremony and reception in the same venue. Many places will not charge a ceremony fee (like a house of worship would) and you can save on the cost of limos. Our wedding venue was a block away from our hotel so the hotel guests and brides arrived on foot.
- Choose flowers that are in season when considering your wedding colors and floral designs. In-season flowers are much less expensive (and don't have the negative environmental impact of those transported from around the world). We used hydrangea and peonies as the primary flowers for our early July wedding.
- Use lots and lots and lots of candles!
- If you want a wedding cake, consider using a decorated "dummy" cake for display and frosted sheet cakes for actual service of your guests. Many cake decorators have beautifully decorated display cakes available for

rental that cost significantly less than a real, decorated cake.

- Cupcakes are cute and quite inexpensive, sometimes as little as one and a half dollars each, instead of the three and a half dollars per slice that's the standard minimum for wedding cakes. Still want a cake-cutting? Order a small nine-inch cake to cut!
- If you have an amazingly articulate, eloquent friend or family member who you would trust to officiate your wedding ceremony, he or she can do so for fifty dollars with a permit from the state. Contrast this cost with the fee of justices of the peace, who charge one hundred fifty dollars and up, and those of rabbis, ministers, and celebrants who often charge five hundred dollars or more.
- Have a family or friend do your hair and makeup.
- True DIYers can save money with homemade centerpieces, handcrafted invitations, and countless other fun DIY projects.
- Go to etsy.com and find small operations that will custom-make everything for you. There are great talents on etsy who make everything from wedding dresses to invitations.
- Finally, I can't forget to remind you of two things: 1) if you're really stressed about money, elope! and 2) hiring a wedding planner such as myself can save you 10 to 20 percent on services like catering, photography, floral design, and more.

Let me conclude by suggesting a few areas in which you should not cut corners in the interest of saving:

- Photography and videography: Long after the food is eaten and the day is over, the images are the things that will remain. If you don't hire a photographer to capture your big day, I promise you'll regret it later.

- Music: See my advice about why you shouldn't use an iPOD!
- Your wardrobe: I want you all to feel like the beautiful brides and grooms you are. Be sure to feel 100 percent comfortable and beautiful in your wedding attire.

# Chapter 16:
# The Look, the Feel, the Flow!

You've reached the stage where your wedding is almost planned. The major logistics are done, the officiant, photographer, videographer, florist, and cake maker are booked. Now, how do you make it look, feel, and flow well? The flow of your event starts with the room where most of your wedding activity will occur. Let's call that room the ballroom, even if it's not.

## Floor Plans

Most brides and grooms don't spend much time thinking about their reception floor plan or room layout. And it's not something that is discussed in many wedding-planning books. And although the floor plan isn't very glamorous, it's a critical element in ensuring a smooth and fun reception, especially if you're having a seated meal rather than a cocktail receptoin. It's all about the flow, and if the room is crowded or your guests are in lines, your guests will notice—and it will drive even the most indifferent of them batty.

## Room Size

Staff members of every venue will know the dimensions of the room. Ask for them and try to get an actual diagram of the space. In particular, note any architectural elements that may interrupt the floor space, such as columns, a stairwell, or a stage. During your site visit, take a note of where the electrical outlets are located. It seems like a lot of work now but you'll be happy for it later. These are all elements of your floor plan!

The good news is that many venues will readily have this information to share. This is an example of a floor plan for a plated dinner wedding with all round tables, a DJ and a sweetheart table for the couple:

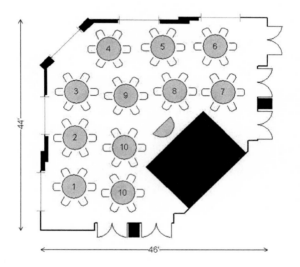

Other dimensions to note:

- Size of the following tables
  - o Cocktail tables (typically 36" round and low, or 24" round and 42" high)
  - o Dinner table (60" round and 72" round tables are standard)
  - o Escort-card table (typically a 36" round table, or a 6' rectangular table)

- o Guest book/Foundation Covenant table (typically a 36" round table, or a 6' rectangular table)
- o Cake table (typically a 24" or 36" round table)
- o Gift table (typically a 6' or 8' rectangular table)
- o Tables for buffet/food stations (typically a 6' or 8' rectangular table)
- o DJ table (typically a 6' or 8' rectangular table)
- Lounge furniture present at the venue, and dimensions
- Space needed behind the buffet or food-stations table
- Space needed behind the DJ table

## The Dinner Tables

Using all of the information gathered above, you can create the actual layout of the room for your wedding day. You can play around with square, round or rectangle tables and see how they all fit together in the space. In a perfect world, the venue will already have this diagram for you. It's important to have all of the elements be to scale so you can rearrange the pieces around the room according to how you want to make the room look.

This could be an exercise in poster board, cardboard, a ruler and markers, or you can use one of the software products available on the market. If you have a wedding planner, he or she probably has this software and can work up a diagram in a matter of minutes.

## Engineering the Room

Now, using the diagram you've created, mark the areas in which people will be coming and going. Where are the high-traffic areas?

Keep in mind that if you're having a cocktail reception rather than a seated meal, most of your guests will be standing anyway and there won't be a need for many dinner tables on the floorplan.

Rearrange the floor plan after you've taken high-traffic areas into account. For example, if you anticipate a long line at the bar, don't position the bar near a dinner table. Keep arranging until you have a flow of the space that minimizes bottlenecks and lines and gives your guests maximum freedom of movement.

Problem areas for lines:

- Receiving line,
- Bar, especially during cocktail hour,
- Stationary food displays set during cocktail hour,
- The buffet/food stations
- The guest book or Foundation Covenant

Keep these tips in mind:

- If you are having a long head table with all members facing forward, place this table against a centrally located wall.
- If you are having a sweetheart table (just the newlyweds), centrally place it in the room, or if the room has a view, place the table in a nice scenic spot.
- If you are seated at a table with your guests (but you're not officially at a head table), place this table in a centrally located area of the room.
- If you are having a cake, it's nice to have it in the middle of the room as long as your guests are not crossing through.
- Ideally, your dance floor should be in the middle of the room with the tables spread around it.
- Set tables four or more feet apart so that guests can move easily and servers can easily pass through to refill water and serve meals.
- Each guest needs about two feet per chair for maximum comfort.

- All wedding announcements and toasts should come from one central area of the room.
- Don't sit older guests near the DJ or band's large blaring speakers.
- Position the bar in a slightly out-of-the-way area that will not disrupt movement.
- If you are having a buffet or food stations, it's ideal to have access from both sides of the table. If you can't have this access, position the tables so that there's very clearly an entrance and an exit to the buffet so your guests don't have to pass through others in line in order to get back to their tables.

## Guests with Special Needs

If you have any guests who are in a wheelchair, who have trouble moving, or who have larger bodies, assign them to a table that won't be in a high-traffic area. You don't want them to have to constantly be moving their chair in order to let other guests pass by.

## Who sits where? How do they know?

Where you will seat your guests is a matter of how formal you want your wedding to be. You have three choices:

1. Free for all. Everyone sits where they want. Please don't do this. Chaos will ensue.
2. Assign each guest to a table.
3. Assign each guest to a table *and* a seat at that table.

If you are *only* assigning each guest a table, you do so in one of the following ways:

## Escort Cards

Escort cards, or seating cards, tell each guest where to sit. These include the guest's name and table name or number. You can use one per couple if you wish, or give each person his or her own. Either is fine.

An escort card will look like this:
*Mr. Jeffrey Jackson and Mr. Daniel Brown*
*Table 12*

Jeffrey and Daniel will pick up their card and look for table 12—the card serves to "escort" them to that table. And once they are at that table, they can sit wherever they want, unless they see a place card.

## Seating Chart

An alternative to a table full of cards is a seating chart. The chart can be a poster board (with your wedding colors or theme, please) listing the table names or numbers and the guests assigned to each.

If you do have a seating chart, make sure it looks great (nice frame helps add elegance), is big enough to read, is in a centrally located place and won't cause a traffic jam.

If you are assigning a guest to a table *and* a seat at that table, you choose one of the above *and also* use place cards.

*Escort cards*

# Place Cards

Place cards are the cards at each place setting that tell guests which seat belongs to them. Guests will then sit in their assigned seat. They are most often placed above the plate facing outward.

*Note regarding catering:*

Bear in mind that your caterer may ask you to use place cards. For example, if you have requested that your guests pre-select an entrée, your caterer may require that you indicate (on a place card) which entrée each guest requested. Note that not all caterers require this; some will ask guests which entrée they chose.

*Place card*

# Chapter 17:
## Designing Your Gay Wedding

Weddings are great way to express your design philosophy! What is your design philosophy? Look around your home and in your closet. Think about your cultural background. Since your wedding is all about celebrating you and your partner, then I urge you to have fun with a color or design theme.

I no longer read many wedding blogs or magazines. It's depressing how similar so many of the images are. If I see one more series of photographs of a wedding in the countryside with flowers on shepherd's hooks, the newlyweds on a bicycle built for two, and a floral display of artfully arranged "weeds," I'm going to pull my hair out. These concepts are no longer original. Your wedding should be as original as you are. And if it's original, it's going to be fabulous.

I suggest that each couple have two to four wedding colors, with one as the primary color and two or three as accent colors. These colors can be carried throughout your gay wedding, beginning with the save-the-date card and all the way through to the wedding cake, table linens, flowers, and so on. Our wedding colors were navy, silver, and white.

For clients who are struggling to decide what colors to use, wedding planners often help them create an inspiration board.

Inspiration boards are essentially a collage of things that you like: they could be colors, objects, and/or themes. The images could come from weddings, from magazines, or from nature. Do a Google images search for "inspiration boards" and you'll see some pop up.

There's a great, new, easy way to create inspiration boards for your wedding—check out MyKateParkerWedding.com and once you're registered, click the Inspiration link. You can chose from colors, seasons, and more, to instantly get the perfect inspiration board for you.

Here are an example of an inspiration board:

Once you've been thoroughly inspired, it's time to move on to the actual design. Although there are other significant elements (such as furniture, stationery, and drapes), I think of basic wedding design in three main areas: floral; tablescapes, (which are creatively designed tables); and lighting.

I talked about floral design already, so in this chapter I'll focus on tablescapes and lighting.

## Tablescapes

If your wedding colors are not white or ivory, why settle for the standard white or ivory linens when you can really give your reception tables some pizzazz? It doesn't have to cost a lot of money. Linens play a big role in creating your desired ambiance for an event. They can tie a room together and give it a cohesive feel. Most venues own linens and can provide standard poly-cotton or plain cotton ivory or white linens. Most of my clients elect to upgrade to something nicer, or to use one of those fabrics but in a more thematic color. Besides flowers, upgrading linens is the single investment that will have the greatest visual impact at your wedding.

## Linen Sizes

Most wedding planners, banquet coordinators and rental companies will be able to tell you the size of linen you'll need the moment you provide them with the table size. But in case you need help with this item, the list below will help you specify size(s) you'll need.

- The standard dinner table is a 60" round table. The linen most commonly used on this table is a 120" linen. This linen goes all the way to the floor.
- The standard small, low table used for cocktails, cake and the sweethearts is a 36" round table. The linen most commonly used to cover this table is a 90" linen.
- The standard high cocktail table is 24" or 36" round and 42" tall. For these tables, we most commonly use a 120" linen.
- Rectangular table sizes vary so check with your venue's banquet coordinator to find out those dimensions.

Also ask him or her about the precise size of other tables that will be used at your event.

## Fabrics

Here are some common fabrics used at weddings:

**Poly-cotton:** Poly-cotton linens come in a large variety of colors and are the most inexpensive way to give color to your space without breaking the bank. They are also good for food stations, the DJ table, the entry table, and other accent tables. These will cost about fifteen dollars each for a 120" solid color.

**Lamour:** Linens made of lamour are shiny and soft to the touch. They cost approximately thirty dollars each for a 120" solid color.

**Bengaline:** Shiny like lamour fabric, bengaline linens have more texture, which is created by a thin ribbing. Expect to spend about thirty each for 120" solid color bengaline linens.

**Bichon:** Bichon linens are shiny but with a crinkly texture. They'll run you about thirty five dollars each for a 120" solid color.

**Pintuck:** Pintuck linens have diamond or square patterns created by seams throughout the fabric. Very fabulous! Pintucks are on the expensive side, costing about thirty five dollars each for a 120" solid color.

To have a sense of how many linens to order for an average wedding with one hundred guests, follow this example (note: this is *only* an example; check with your wedding planner, caterer, or venue for the actual specs you'll be using):

- Twelve round dinner tables (120" round)
- Five high cocktail tables (120" round)
- One DJ table (132" round)
- One escort-card table (132" round)
- One Foundation Covenant/gift table (132" round)
- One cake table (108" round)
- One stationary hors d'oeuvre table (132" round)
- One bar table (132" round)

The totals in this example come to:

- Seventeen 120" rounds
- Five 132"rounds
- One 108" round

Depending on the fabric you choose and where you order from, in the example above your linen rental cost could vary from four hundred dollars to nine hundred dollars and up, not including tax and delivery fees.

Table runners are very popular right now and can be placed across the base linen as an accent. Table runners will give your table some contrast, sophistication, and textural depth. If you're crafty (or willing to try), I've seen some cute DIY table-runner ideas recently. They can be made from discount fabrics, wallpaper, or whatever your imagination will allow. With fabric scissors, an iron, and stitch witchery, you can make your tables pop. There are also some really cute runners for sale on Etsy.com if you're looking for someone else's handmade designs!

*A beautifully designed tablescape.*

# Napkins

Don't overlook the napkins! Some linens have matching napkins, but often you'll use a poly-cotton napkin in the closest color you can find. There are a variety of napkin folds, such as the one in the photo above. I'm a big fan of napkin rings as an accessory and a rolled napkin as an elegant touch to the tablescape.

For cocktail hour, if your caterer would normally provide boring cocktail napkins, you can affordably upgrade with something customized. You can order monogrammed and other personalized napkins from a site such as www.Beau-Coup.com. I love this simple touch that shows that you've thought about the details!

## China, Stemware, and Flatware

Once have the base in place, you'll start to add the elements that sit on top of the linens: the china, stemware, and flatware. If your wedding venue will be providing food and beverage, be sure to ask to see its standard setting. You can always upgrade to something more suitable. If you are bringing in your own caterer and rental items, you should ask to see samples so you can find the combination that best expresses your wedding vision.

If you have the ability to do so, you can include crystal (instead of glass) stemware, silver flatware (instead of stainless), and interesting china. Chargers are another beautiful addition to a tablescape that can add some whimsy, elegance, or color, depending on what look you are going for. While I don't like to waste paper, I've even seen fun paper chargers/placemats. Many of these items can be rented at your local party-rental business.

Add to all this stunningly cohesive and complementary place cards and menus, and you will have a gorgeous tablescape!

## Chairs

We've all been to ballrooms where the standard chair is something that's not quite wedding-appropriate, looking more suitable for an eight-hour corporate meeting (and in fact designed for that purpose.) Sure, you can use those chairs at your wedding but will they fit the overall look you seek?

*Ugly hotel chairs*

You can cover them up with chair covers...

Most clients I've worked with don't bother covering the standard ugly banquet chairs with (nearly as tacky!) chair covers, but instead bring in new chairs altogether.

The most common chair style, by far, is the Ballroom or Chiavari Chair. Available in a wide variety of colors and seat-pad colors, it can match any décor. It's elegant, sturdy, and comfortable, and you can rent them for about seven dollars each.

*Chiavari Chair*

But seven dollars per chair can add up and if you choose to use chair covers instead, those are about four dollars each. While not as elegant as the Chiavari chair, they are certainly better than those ugly banquet chairs.

*Garden chairs are most suitable for an outdoor wedding and are rented for about $4 each.*

## It's All in the Lighting

First of all, why use lighting design for your wedding? Great lighting creates a mood. It can be virtually any color to match your theme. It can hide ugly walls. It creates ambiance and intimacy. It's romantic. Special lighting is no longer very expensive, and it can save you money in other areas (such as on flowers, perhaps). Here are some examples of the possible kinds of professional lighting.

## Uplighting

Uplights are placed on the floor and radiate color upward. Simple enough. You may have seen uplights at an event and not even noticed them. If, in the past, you've attended a wedding or an event with professional lighting design, you may have noticed some wires and some big black boxes on the floor (radiating heat), covered with a sheet of colored plastic. That's an old-school method but it's still a very effective way of lighting a space. In fact, in some cases, that method of uplighting a room is the most advantageous.

Today's uplights are often wireless, and professionals use LED lights, rather than canned lights. These wireless lights are, of course, wireless, and they also don't emit heat. As an added benefit, these types of lights are remote controlled, so the color of the light can literally change with the push of a button. Very cool! They're also lightweight, and can easily be placed around the room (and later moved if necessary). Another advantage of LED uplights is that they're easy to install, meaning lower labor costs. This can be a very cost effective way to design your ballroom.

## Centerpiece Uplights

Centerpiece uplights have a small base that the centerpiece sits on. The base lights up into the clear glass centerpiece creating a really cool effect on the floral design.

Some small LED lights are waterproof and can actually be submerged into your glass centerpiece container, creating a beautiful glow!

## Paper Lanterns

Most often seen in tents, paper lanterns can be strung across any ceiling structure or a structure with a drop ceiling. The traditional method involves electrical wire providing light to the lanterns and keeping them suspended. I know a company that can hang and light lanterns wirelessly from any tent or venue with a drop ceiling. It's a fairly easy setup and thus less expensive than other types of lighting. Paper lanterns are great for adding a casual, fun atmosphere at the wedding.

## Monogram projection

Your wedding logo or monogram can be projected onto the dance floor using either a projector or gobo setup. This is a very traditional look but I love the way it appears in wedding photos!

Lighting transforms spaces and can create a feeling that's so romantic, so intimate, and warm. It's a great investment in your wedding design. If you simply upgrade your linens and add some form of lighting design, you'll instantly have a chic wedding.

## Pipe and Drape

Have you ever walked into a function room and wanted the emergency exit sign or the ugly wallpaper to disappear? The most common way to do this is by using pipe and drape.

Pipe can be put together to cover anything from ten to hundreds of linear feet. Your wedding planner or florist should be able to assemble the pipe that's eight feet high, but for large ballrooms with huge ceilings, you can get pipe that literally goes to the roof—but that must be professionally installed by decorators.

The drape can be a basic white or black cloth, or it can be a beautiful sheer fabric that matches your wedding colors. With pipe and drape, your ballroom is not limited by its original design: it can literally be anything you want it to be. Pipe and drape creates texture and depth, and brings elegance and intimacy to a space. It can change directions every ten linear feet, so you can literally create walls or sections in a large room.

Basic pipe and drape in a standard solid color that you, your friends, or your nice wedding planner sets up costs about thirty dollars per ten-foot section. The prices go up from there.

Pipe and drape plus uplights were used to create an intimate space that became a lounge for the wedding guests.

## Entertaining Your Guests

Have I mentioned that we had a surprise guest at our wedding, and that she was *fierce*? Jen took the mic and introduced our surprise guest after our strawberry-shortcake cutting. Her name is Mizery, and she's Boston's most legendary drag queen.

Jen felt strongly that we needed to give our wedding an extra bit of *oomph* to entertain our guests. Above all, she did not want a boring wedding. I was thinking we'd hire a fire dancer, but Jen often gets her way and is usually right, so we hired Mizery. Well, our wedding certainly wasn't boring, and as Jen promised when she introduced Mizery, the party was about to get started.

Mizery performed "We are Family" and got some guests up and dancing with her—and then she did a split! You had to see it to believe it. The look on our guests' faces was priceless and people are still talking about it.

Mizery added a little bit of fabulousness to *our* wedding, but I've also had clients hire a fire dancer, tango dancers, flamenco performers, and the like. You get the drift … little bit of entertainment (and I do meet a short piece) goes a long way toward creating wedding memories.

*Mizery at our wedding*

## The Art of the Toast

I've planned so many weddings at this point that I have excellent instincts about the art of wedding production. One of the "rules" I have for most couples is: two to four toasts, max. Designate articulate and funny individuals to toast in advance. Tell your DJ or wedding coordinator who is toasting. When I'm in charge, I'll schedule the time for the toasts and cue the toast accordingly so that the caterer, photographer, videographer and DJ or band are all ready for them. I urge you to discourage "open-mic" toasts. Keep the toasts to less than five minutes each. Keep them clean. Simple enough, right?

Occasionally, rules are meant to be broken, and I'm absolutely thrilled that my clients from a recent wedding broke my rules for toasting. These gentlemen who live in Manhattan brought about fifty friends and family from literally around the world to Boston to celebrate their wedding. It was a beautiful, classy wedding, with live Brazilian jazz all evening.

Throughout the amazing three-course meal, there were toasts—eleven in all, starting and ending with the grooms. I have to say that those eleven people were among the funniest, sweetest, most generous and affectionate toasters I have ever heard. Which was not at all surprising, because the grooms are funny, sweet, generous, and affectionate, and it was only fitting that they would have such a great community of friends and family. So eleven toasts, all brilliant, and everyone had an amazing time.

I should add that it's become a gay-wedding tradition for the brides or grooms to toast each other and their guests. Jen and I toasted our guests with mead, based off the Celtic mead toasting tradition but updated, of course, for our gay wedding.

## Personalizing Your Wedding

As you think through these tips and options, keep in mind that it's your wedding, your day. It can be as personal as you wish. A lot of my clients display photos of themselves at the wedding venue.

It's your day and it should be a perfect reflection of your love. How perfect to have photos!

Here are some more areas in which your wedding can be personalized.

## Wedding-Cake Toppers

Many of my clients have not had cake toppers on their wedding cake. It's your prerogative. Unless you shop online you may have difficulty finding LGBT cake toppers in your local bakeries. However, you can find some good resources for custom-made cake toppers that look just like you! A quick Internet search will reveal some good resources. I also recommend www.GayWeddings.com and some vendors on www.Etsy.com.

*Two leather bear grooms put two bears atop their cake.*

*Custom cake topper designed to look like the brides.*

*One couple added a little bit of whimsy to their cake.*

*Two porcelain brides made for a more traditional cake topper.*

## Guest Books

As mentioned in Chapter 11, many gay couples have their guests sign a Foundation Covenant instead of a guest book. In my experience, guest books usually end up with only a few pages written on, and many blank pages. I don't really like them or recommend them. When thinking about a guest book, I try to imagine where it will be stored after the wedding. When will you look at it again? Will it just be collecting dust somewhere? One of the reasons I like the Foundation Covenant so much is that it's framed and hung on the wall. With that idea in mind, here are a few other creative guest book ideas:

- **Recipe for love:** Guests write their recipe for love on an index card and place it in a recipe box that you'll later keep in your kitchen.
- **Coffee-table book:** At any bookstore, buy a hard-cover high quality coffee-table book on your choice of topics (preferably one you'll find interesting for years to come) and let guests write on the pages.
- **Engravable photo mats or serving platter:** There is a company online, IDoEngravables.com that sells photo mats, serving platters, and other items made of stainless steel that can be written on with a special pen Your guests sign the serving platter and then it's yours, forever, with a great reminder of your wedding day.

## Napkin Rings

Napkin rings can be totally superfluous, but they can also be a beautiful tablescape accessory. I love how napkin rings can give a tiny bit of extra punch to a place setting. If you can afford them or have some mad DIY skills, then by all means, go for personalized napkin rings. Paloma's Nest is a company I referred to earlier when talking about ring-bearer bowls; they also make very cool napkin rings.

## Garters

To be honest, I've never seen a gay wedding with a garter toss, but I do think it's a fun tradition and of course, I've had several brides wear garters. If you are interested in wedding garters, I highly recommend the collection by Julianne Smith, a DC-based designer of custom-made and stylish wedding garters. There can be elements of your parent's wedding incorporated, your favorite sports team, hobby, or anything else that has meaning to you. Julianne's collection is at www.TheGarterGirl.com

## Favors

In my opinion, favors should be done right or not at all! Go big or go home! After cleaning up after countless weddings where favors are left behind by guests enjoying themselves on the dance floor, I really believe that in general, they're a waste.

That said, I've found the most successful favors are edible! Give guests a delicious truffle or chocolate-covered strawberry and it'll be gone, sometimes before the end of the night! Some edible favors can be packaged in such a way that the fold can double as an escort-card holder. In this case, the favor is placed on an escort-card table and guests bring it to their seat.

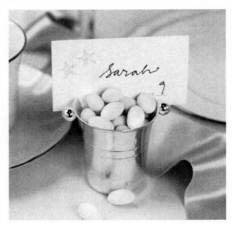

Guests' names are on each favor, and the favors are set up as an escort-card display.

Another way to make sure that favors get distributed is to have them passed to guests as they exit. In the same way that guests are passed champagne when they arrive, favors can be butler-passed on nice serving trays as guests leave. So classy!

# DIY

DIY stands for "Do It Yourself." I'll be the first to admit that I'm *not* a crafty person and not at all capable of DIY projects. Some people, however (including of course, Martha Stewart), are brilliant. There are some wonderful DIY resources you should check out to help you make napkin rings, guest books, escort cards, place cards, table runners, linens, and other wedding accessories. If you have the time, energy, and inclination to make a go at some DIY projects, I highly recommend the following Web sites for templates and step-by-step instructions:

- www.DIYBride.com
- www.MarthaStewartWeddings.com
- www.WeddingChicks.com

And if you, like me, are not a DIY master (but you still appreciate the handcrafted look), you'll find many cool wedding accessories for sale on www.Etsy.com. I know that I recommended this site earlier in the book, but I think it's worth a second mention. Etsy is a great place where crafters sell their wares and can even create custom products just for you. I've had some good experience with Etsy vendors, but be sure to read reviews and find out for yourself. On Etsy, you can find anything from napkin rings to aisle runners to invitations to wedding wardrobe. The variety is truly astounding!

# Chapter 18:
# Tying it Together Before You Tie the Knot

Two to four weeks prior to your wedding, you and your partner should sit down and write down the answers to the following questions:

- Are you staying at a hotel the night of the wedding?
- Do you have any guests with disabilities or special needs?
- Will there be a printed program for the ceremony? Who is making this?
- Who are you designating to distribute the program at the wedding?
- Do you want a rehearsal? When will it be held?
- Will there be any drinks passed before ceremony? What kinds? Has the caterer taken responsibility for providing these beverages?
- How important is starting the ceremony on time? What's the latest you want to start?
- Is there a certain side you want families and friends to sit on? (ie. Kelly's side and Jen's side)

- Who are you designating (mother, attendant, etc.) to answer vendor questions on your wedding day so you don't have to be bothered?
- Will you require ushers? Who are you designating to do this?
- Is anyone being escorted?
- Where are you walking in from (back, sides)? Are you walking in together?
- Will you be setting up any special seating for ceremony (for example, a circle, semi-circle, aisles, and the like)?
- Do you want any reserved seating? If so, any special kinds of reserved signs? Who will provide and place these signs?
- Do you have any restrictions (such as no photos taken during the ceremony, or no confetti)?
- When do you want music to be cued during the ceremony? What is the processional song? What is the recessional song?
- Who are you designating to pin personal flowers? Some couples like to involve friends in tasks like this.
- Do you plan to have a receiving line? When will it be held?
- Are you having a seating chart, escort cards or place cards? Do you want the name cards arrayed in a certain way? Where would you like these to be placed?
- Do you want a guest book? Where do you want this placed?
- Do you want any special formal photos taken (for example, special group shots or photos of parents)?

Use the answers to each question to build out a task list. For example, if you haven't thought about ushers, add that to your list of things to do.

# The Wedding Weekend

Gay marriage isn't legal in many places, so many of my clients live in other states and when I'm planning their wedding, I plan a whole weekend's worth of activities. These activities might include a welcome reception the night the guests arrive, a tourist activity the day of the wedding, the wedding itself, and a brunch the following day. Even when the couple doesn't live in another state, guests often travel in from all over for the wedding.

For many people, a wedding is the first time that an entire family has been together in years and the event serves as a family reunion. Some will say that a wedding is the only time that all of the people you love will be in the same place at the same time. That's part of the point, isn't it? To declare your love and commitment in front of all of your favorite witnesses?

If you have everyone all in one place, might as well make a weekend out of it, right?

# The Wedding Rehearsal

You have to have a wedding rehearsal.

Even if it's only fifteen minutes long, do it. Take the time to do a dry run so that you have fewer nerves on your wedding day.

**Who to invite:** For your rehearsal, invite the person marrying you, the wedding party, parents, grandparents, and readers. If possible, any musicians who will play at the ceremony should also attend. Do not invite anyone not involved in the wedding to the rehearsal, as they'll be distracting. This is not the time to be social!

**Who's in charge:** The officiant is in charge of the rehearsal, unless you have a wedding planner.

**When:** Preferably, the rehearsal should take place during the late afternoon or early evening before your wedding. Tip! Tell those who are invited to show up fifteen to thirty minutes before you actually want the rehearsal to start. Some rehearsals are quite complex and it's hard to catch up if you're running late!

**Where:** If possible, rehearse at your ceremony site. If you absolutely cannot use that location, I like small hotel function rooms and backyards as back-up locations. But be sure to let all those coming know where it is!

**How:** If possible, arrange to have the room at least partly set up for the rehearsal so the processional and recessional can be accurately rehearsed and so everyone will know where to stand. If you are using a unity candle or Foundation Covenant, be sure to have a table set up by the ceremony site. If you are using a chuppah, it would be ideal to have this pre-set as well.

**Tip:** meet your bridal party the night before or earlier in the day before the rehearsal so you can all go to the rehearsal together and no one will be late!

## The Rehearsal Dinner

A trend I've seen lately is to invite to the rehearsal dinner all of the traveling guests who are in town on the night before the wedding. That's up to you, but that decision can balloon a twenty-person rehearsal dinner to a forty-person rehearsal dinner. Double the number of guests and you double the budget.

In a traditional bride and groom scenario, the rehearsal dinner is hosted by the grooms' parents. You can make whatever arrangements work for you. The couple sometimes hosts, or one of the parents do, or it's a shared endeavor. But one way or another, it's nice to feed people. A rehearsal dinner need not be a formal affair. Sometimes it's a cookout or a potluck. Choose an option that fits your budget and makes the most sense for you.

We decided only to invite those in our immediately family and in the wedding party to the rehearsal dinner. We had about twenty guests. We wanted to create a casual, informal feel so our rehearsal dinner was a gourmet pizza and salad buffet. The food was delicious and it was light and easy.

# The Welcome Reception

Instead of a rehearsal dinner, many of my clients host a welcome reception-cocktail party for all the guests visiting. It's very informal, short (only about two hours) and often in the host hotel. There are usually no toasts and nothing structured. It's just a fun way to catch up with your wedding guests who have come from all over to be with you.

# The Post-Rehearsal Dinner Party

To avoid the awkwardness of accommodating guests from out of town who arrive to your wedding location the night before the event, you should invite everyone to meet you at a central location for a casual get together. For example, on the logistics card of our wedding invitation, we had a section that said:

Friday, July 2, 2009: At 8:00 PM, please join us for live Irish music and drinks at Mr. Dooley's Irish Pub [address]

This type of casual, welcoming invite does not obligate you to host this secondary event, but provides a common and casual meeting place for wedding guests.

Just don't stay out too late or drink too much the night before your wedding!

# The Post-Wedding Brunch

Even if you've already flown off on your honeymoon, the post-wedding brunch is another way to give wedding guests from out of town a way to be entertained.

Often, this brunch is hosted by the parents of the bride or groom, but the trend is to have it hosted by no one. Many couples simply spread the word verbally or include information in the guests' hotel welcome bag to meet for brunch at 10:00 AM in the hotel restaurant.

It's a painless and simple way to plan a brunch, and there's no financial obligation. And if you are, in fact, still around, your guests will appreciate seeing you again.

## Tourist Activities

If your wedding is somewhere that is a true "destination"—that is, somewhere your guests may enjoy being tourists or exploring—then it would be generous of you to provide them with a list of things to do. This could be as simple as typing up a bulleted list, to researching pricing and phone numbers. You can also include local tourist information and maps, which are easily obtained at any hotel. You are under no obligation to set up tours, arrange meals or purchase tickets.

As mentioned in the chapter on involving your parents, I'd advise that you delegate this task to a parent. It's one less thing for you to do and one more way to channel a parent's energy.

## The Wedding Schedule

Below is a sample schedule from a real wedding. I created this in Microsoft Excel. If you don't have a wedding coordinator who will create a schedule for you, I'd suggest going through the exercise of creating a schedule yourself. It's important to make sure that you (and preferably, not your friends or family) are not in charge of these tasks on your wedding day. Hopefully you'll have a Day of Coordinator or competent venue manager who can handle these tasks.

Your vendors should each receive a copy of this schedule so they can be aware of who is doing what and when. The staff at your venue should also receive a copy.

You'll notice at the bottom of the schedule, I include a list of balances due, suggested tips, and things to pack.

**Jody and Beth Wedding Schedule Draft**
**14 Conway Rod, Boston, MA**
**122 adults for dinner; 128 for ceremony**

| Time | Activity | Who |
|------|----------|-----|
| 10am-12pm | Be Our Guest drops off rentals | Be Our Guest |
| 12pm | Jody arrives at 14 Conway Road<br>Makeup artist Julie arrives at 14 Conway Road | Jody; Julie |
| 12:30pm | Hair lady Deb arrives | Deb |

| Time | Tasks | Who |
|---|---|---|
| 12:30pm | Bernadette, Jen and Ki arrive at 220 Dudley Rd for setup. Tasks include:<br>*set up 2 pathways (one that guests will travel upon arrival/departure; the other to the portapotty trailer) using shepherd's hooks, hanging candle lanterns with live candles; and LED candles at the base.<br>*set up white balloons at entrance to Dudley Rd & entrance to #220, driveway<br>*set up clothesline with escort cards on clothes pins near the bar<br>*in the cocktail hour area, set up table with recipe box, cards and chalk board - chalk board to say "Please share your favorite recipe for love with Jody and Beth"<br>*stake signs directing guests up toward the restrooms & place LED candles at the base<br>*set up hand lotion and soap in the bathroom<br>*set up table numbers according to the diagram provided by the couple<br>*set up ceremony chairs with first row reserved, marked by ribbon and sign<br>*set up ceremony altar: lantern on left, hurricane and accessories on back, center; tea pot in front left center; bowl on front right center; floral arrangement on the far right<br>*place one camera on each guest table<br>*turn off pool filter<br>*tape off pool filter<br>*place wedding favors at each place setting<br>*place a few votives on each dinner table<br>*set up candy bar<br>*set up votives in the restroom<br>*place table numbers on each table<br>*create sacred space in ceremony area using the heart stones<br>*pick up any branches if necessary, clear up the pathways | Bernadette, Jen and Ki |

| Time | Task | Person/Vendor |
|---|---|---|
| 1pm | Caterer arrives and begins setup, supervised by Bernadette:<br>*set up dinner tables<br>*set up cocktail tables<br>*create kitchen area | Above and Beyond, Bernadette |
| 1pm | Gordon's Liquors drops off alcohol | Gordon's |
| 1pm | DJ Melissa Lyons arrives for setup | Kristin |
| 1:30pm | Florist arrives and begins setup supervised by Bernadette:<br>*begins with placing floating candles and flowers in the pool<br>*altar area<br>*centerpieces<br>*empty vase for bouquet on sweetheart table<br>*hands off personal flowers<br>*cocktail tables | Bernadette, Kelly |
| 2pm | Valet company arrives for setup | Paul is the supervisor |
| 2:30pm | Photographer arrives and takes a few final getting ready photos | Susan |

| | | |
|---|---|---|
| 2:30pm | Chamber Players arrive for setup and Bernadette directs them accordingly | Carol, Bernadette |
| 2:45pm | Ki takes his place as greeter near front of the house | Ki |
| 3pm | Barbara the videographer arrives | Barbara |
| 3pm | Andy from Sperry arrives to troubleshoot | Andy |
| 3pm | Guests begin to arrive, are greeted and directed by Ki and prosecco is passed by caterer | Guests |
| 3pm | Rev. Farrah arrives | Rev Farrah |
| 3:20pm | Guests are encouraged to take their seats for the ceremony | Jen and Ki |
| 3:23pm | Bernadette retrieves Beth. Beth and Farrah take their places | Bernadette, Beth, Farrah |
| 3:25pm | Ki unfurls the aisle runner | Ki |

| Time | Description | Responsible |
|---|---|---|
| 3:27pm | Bernadette retrieves Jody from the house with her brother Jeff and lines up the processional coming from around the tent<br>1. Flower girl Ava<br>2. Jody escorted by Jeff (Jody on the left) | Bernadette, Jody, Jeff, Ava |
| 3:30pm | Bernadette cues Carol/string trio to play processional "Canon D" | Bernadette |
| 3:30pm | Processional begins | |
| 3:50pm | Ceremony interlude from "Les Miserables," 30 seconds after the announcement of silent prayer and meditation | Carol |
| 4:15pm | Ceremony concludes, recessional begins "Trumpet Tune and March" | |
| 4:15pm | Bernadette brings Jody a Malibu + Pineapple and Beth a drink TBD | Carol |
| 4:20pm | Guests move to cocktail hour; hors d'oeuvres passed | Above and Beyond |

| | | Photographer |
|---|---|---|
| 4:20pm | Formal photos:<br>Jody and Beth<br>Jody and Beth + Jeff<br>Jody and Beth + Norma and Anthony<br>Jody and Beth + Ava<br>Jody and Beth + Caulders<br>Jody and Beth + entire family<br>Bart + William + Fred<br>Beth + Norma, Bart, William and Fred<br>Beth + Caulders<br>Beth + entire family<br>Beth and Jeannie<br>Beth + Norma and Anthony<br>Beth + Anthony<br>Beth + Tony and Anthony<br>Beth + Tony, Anthony and Norma<br>Beth + Jeff<br>Jody + Sandi, Stanley and Eric<br>Jody + Jeff and Colleen<br>Jody + Jeff<br>Jody + Sandi<br>Jody + Tomoco<br>Jody + Michael<br>Jody + Patricia<br>Jody + Patricia + Michael | |

| Time | Action | People |
|---|---|---|
| 4:25pm | *Bernadette, Jen and Ki move chairs to dinner tables<br>*Move cocktail table with parent photo & flowers under the tent<br>*String trio moves to pool area | Bernadette, Jen and Ki trio |
| 5:15pm | Bernadette, Jen and Ki usher guests into tent for dinner | Bernadette, Jen and Ki |
| 5:20pm | Guests are seated for dinner | |
| 5:22pm | Bernadette brings Jody and Beth to the tent for introductions and first dance. Bernadette cues DJ for introductions, "I'd like to now introduce the newlyweds Jody and Beth" and the first dance song "As" | DJ, Jody and Beth, Bernadette |
| 5:30pm | Jody and Beth are seated for dinner | Jody and Beth |
| 5:32pm | Cued by Bernadette and announced by DJ, welcome to guests by Beth | DJ Kristin, Beth, Bernadette |
| 5:35pm | Bernadette, Jen and Ki:<br>*move the cocktail table arrangements to the restroom<br>*move the recipe-card table to inside the tent | Bernadette, Jen and Ki |

| Time | Description | Who |
|---|---|---|
| 5:50pm | After first course is served, first round of toasts (drinks in hand), announced by DJ and cued by Bernadette who delivers mic to Norma:<br>1. Norma<br>2. Jeff | DJ |
| 6:20pm | After second course is served, second round of toasts, announced by DJ and cued by Bernadette:<br>1. Michael | DJ |
| 6:40pm | After second course is cleared, DJ announces cake cutting, immediately moving into the second dance "When Love Takes Over." | DJ, Jody and Beth |
| 7:00pm | Dessert, cake and candy bar is open | |
| 8:55pm | DJ to announce that guests whose birthday is nearest at each table can take the centerpiece. DJ also announces "Please be sure to share your recipe for love with Jody and Beth" | DJ Kristin |
| 9pm | Wedding ends; breakdown begins. Tasks include:<br>*leftover open liquor goes inside house<br>*recipe box, chalkboard, disposable cameras, Hansen parents' photo, lantern moved inside the house<br>*gifts to Bernadette's car<br>*tables, chairs and linens broken down<br>*shepherds hooks and candles to Bernadette's car | |

# Your Wedding-Day Packing List

Make a packing list and assign one of you to be responsible for it. Keep updating it. You'll need this or you'll go crazy on the days leading up to your wedding. This is a big little detail. You'll notice that in the sample, one of the packing lists is for the couple and one is for me. In this instance, the couple had given me some items to bring over in advance, I was lending them some of my supplies, and I had some things made for them.

Emergency Kit: If you hired a wedding coordinator, you won't have to worry about any of this stuff because coordinators are all trained to carry emergency kits. If you didn't, take notes and head to CVS, because it's time to stock up on some emergency essentials. These are the bare essentials - a good wedding coordinator will actually carry many more items:

- First aid kit: a travel-sized kit is fine, but you should make sure there's one onsite. Check with the venue's event coordinator or with your caterer, and if they don't have a first aid kit, buy one yourself.
- Advil, Tylenol and antacid tablets: for aches, pains, and upset bellies (again, just in case)
- Hairspray/ hair gel
- Tissues
- Deodorant
- Small mirror
- Plenty of extra bobby pins
- Breath mints
- Clear nail polish - for pantyhose runs and last minute touch ups.
- Shoeshine sponge
- Sewing kit (make sure there's plenty of black and white thread)
- Extra pair of black socks/nylons

- Extra copy of the phone numbers and contact names of all vendors and wedding party members
- Extra copy of the wedding day timeline.
- Extra copy of directions to ceremony and reception sites.

This is one of those tasks that doesn't need to be done last minute. If you're three months out from your wedding day and looking for a project, this is a good one to take care of.

| Jody and Beth's packing list | Bernadette's packing list |
|---|---|
| Votives for tables | Signage |
| Lotion and soap | Stakes |
| Lantern | Clothes line |
| Favors | Clothes pins |
| Jody's parents photo | Shepherd's hooks |
| Escort cards | Candles |
| Recipe box | Candle holders |
| Chalk board | White balloons |
| Tea pot | Balloon string |
| Bowl | Balloon tank |
| Candy for candy bar | Aisle runner |
| Marriage license | Table #s |
| Shoes | Chalk |
| Tea | Ribbon for ceremony chairs |
| Table assignments | Reserved signs |
| Heart shaped stones | LED candles |
| | Lighter |
| | Mallet |
| | Table # holders |
| | Earpieces |
| | Hammer |
| | nails for signage |
| | extension cords |
| | masking tape |
| | Flashlights |
| | Stakes for runner |
| | Menus |

| Vendors | Balance | Cash tip amount |
|---|---|---|
| String Trio | $83 | $100 |
| Florist | paid | $50 |
| Caterer | Credit card will be charged for $9,303.10 | $600 |
| Tent | paid | 0 |
| Liquor | CC will be charged | 0 |
| Hair | $300 | 20% |
| Makeup | $350 | 20% |
| Rev Farrah | $250 | $100 |
| Portapotty rental | paid | 0 |
| Valet Parkers | CC will be charged | 0 |
| Photographer | $997.50 | 0 |
| Videographer | $300 (balance due opon delivery of images) | |
| DJ | paid | 0 |

# Chapter 19:
## Your Lives Together

Congratulations! The deed is done! The knot is tied! The threshold is crossed! And off you go into the first day of the rest of your lives. It's an exciting time for any couple.

But before you get too excited, there's some boring but necessary paperwork I highly recommend you take care of…

## Protecting Your Family

I'm a big fan of making sure that your gay or lesbian family is protected. Once you're married, be aware that your marriage may not be recognized when you travel or even within your own state. Your marriage is not recognized by the U.S. federal government.

While basic estate planning, involving simple joint ownership of assets, may solve some problems and avoid costly, time-consuming probate issues, estate planning for same-sex couples requires additional care. Transfers of property to an opposite-sex spouse are fully exempted from both federal estate and gift taxes, but since the IRS uses the federal definition of marriage, this exemption does not apply to same-sex couples.

Even if property is held jointly, the IRS includes the entire value of the property in the estate of the first owner to die, unless the surviving owner can provide evidence of contribution to the acquisition of the property; this issue does not exist for married opposite-sex couples.

You need to take extra steps to protect your family. Here are the types of documents that you should have prepared for you. It's important to have these documents prepared by an attorney who specializes in family law and who can speak directly to you about legal protections for same-sex families.

## Wills

Wills, generally considered relatively simple tools for distributing an estate's assets, can also define relationships, present evidence of intent, direct guardianship, and much more. Wills for same-sex spouses need not be dramatically different from the wills of heterosexual spouses, but they *can* provide special protections. Having a will in place should be a priority for any same-sex couple, young or old.

## Health Care Proxies

We have all heard horror stories of same-sex spouses excluded from decisions about a spouse's care, treated like strangers by medical professionals, and prevented from visiting by a spouse's blood relatives. A health care proxy is a legal document written to clearly ensure this does not happen to your family and is something you should bring with you every time you travel.

## Durable Power of Attorney

Like all couples, same-sex couples want to act as one: to be able to represent one another and make decisions on each other's behalf. For same-sex couples, however, there is the added importance of recognition across state lines. Even if a couple is married in Massachusetts, Connecticut, Vermont, New Hampshire, Washington D.C., or Iowa, transacting business beyond state lines on behalf of a same-sex spouse may not be possible without a valid Durable Power of Attorney (DPOA).

Jen and I have all of our ducks in a row and all of these documents with the help of a fantastic attorney who specializes in protecting same-sex families. While it is an extra step, the peace of mind these documents provide (especially when we have a child) is priceless. The information contained above was re-printed with permission from our attorney, Claire DeMarco from Brisk Elder Law.

## After the Vows

Getting married is a huge step in any relationship, and as a pretty recent newlywed myself, I can say with confidence that you're going to love being married! For Jen and I, being married just made sense. Being together is the most natural thing in the world.

After our wedding, we went on a honeymoon and came back and crashed. We crashed hard! My life as a wedding planner is pretty intense about eight months a year and our own wedding fell smack dab in the middle of typical wedding season, so I personally was exhausted from planning my own – and other people's – weddings. Our honeymoon in Aruba was exactly what we needed.

But then, we experienced what many couples experience – post-wedding blues. If you think about it, there's so much anticipation prior to your big day. You may have the weight of the world on your shoulders. Wedding talk may dominate your conversations at work, with friends and with your partner. Now that the wedding's over, what is there to talk about?! I'm kidding – hopefully you'll find *something* – but there does tend to be a void. That's exactly what we and many other couples experienced. Fair warning! It's not so large a void that you shouldn't have a wedding. The wedding is *so* worth it!

You know the rhyme, "first comes love, then comes marriage, then comes the baby in the baby carriage." For same-sex couples, as gay weddings are normalized and become more common, this is what happens with many families. We fall in love, we marry (now legally, in some places), and then some of us have kids. It's exciting.

By the time you're reading this book, Jen and I will have a little baby. Jen is pregnant and due in October 2010 and we're thrilled about it. Wish us luck on our new big adventure. I wish you all the best in whatever the future has in store for your family.

# Appendix 1:
## Resources

Gay Wedding Planning Resources:
- 14Stories.com
- Gay.Weddings.com
- GayWeddings.com
- PurpleUnions.com
- QueerlyWed.com
- SoYoureEnGAYged.com

General Wedding Planning Resources:
- MyKateParkerWedding.com
- WeddingChicks.com
- WeddingWire.com

Do It Yourself Project Resources:
- AlbumBoutique.com
- DIYBride.com
- MarthaStewartWeddings.com
- WeddingChicks.com

Green Weddings:

- CottonBride.com
- GetConscious.com
- GreenBrideGuide.com
- Eco-BeautifulWeddings.com

Invitations:
- GayWeddings.com
- OsloPress.com
- OutVite.com
- PapeterieStore.com
- ScissorPaperStone.us
- WeddingPaperDivas.com

Wedding Accessories:
- Beau-Coup.com (favors and other decorative items)
- Etsy.com (all things handcrafted)
- IDoEngravables.com (as a guest book substitute)
- ModernKetubah.com (for the Foundation Covenant and ketubahs)
- PalomasNest.com (for ring bearer bowls and napkin rings)
- TheGarterGirl.com (for stylish wedding garters)

Legal:
- GLAD, GLAD.org
- Lambda Legal, LambdaLegal.org
- Brisk Elder Law, BriskElderLaw.com

Advocacy:
- Human Rights Campaign, HRC.org
- National Center for Lesbian Rights, NCLRights.org
- National Gay and Lesbian Task Force, NGLTF.org

Media:
GLAAD, www.GLAAD.org

# Photograph Acknowledgements

Closed Circle Photography
Gretje Ferguson
Derek Goodwin
Katje Hempel
Marilyn Humphries
Infinity Portrait Design
Michael Manning
Stephanie Martin
Jackie Ricciardi

LaVergne, TN USA
03 February 2011
215155LV00002B/18/P